Health Education

Health Education

M. Dash
Neena Dash

ATLANTIC
PUBLISHERS & DISTRIBUTORS (P) LTD

Published by

ATLANTIC

PUBLISHERS & DISTRIBUTORS (P) LTD

B-2, Vishal Enclave, Opp. Rajouri Garden,
New Delhi-110027
Phones : +91-11-25413460, 25429987, 25466842

Sales Office
7/22, Ansari Road, Darya Ganj,
New Delhi-110002
Phones : +91-11-23273880, 23275880, 23280451
Fax : +91-11-23285873
web : www.atlanticbooks.com
e-mail : info@atlanticbooks.com

Branch Office
5, Nallathambi Street, Wallajah Road,
Chennai-600002
Phones : +91-44-64611085, 32413319
e-mail : chennai@atlanticbooks.com

Printed in India
at Nice Printing Press, Delhi

Preface

The World Health Organisation (WHO) defines health as "a state of complete physical, mental and social well-being, and not merely the absence of disease or infirmity." Good health means the proper functioning of the physique, the chemique, and the psychique, i.e. physical parts of the body, chemical reactions inside the body, and the harmonious functions of the body, respectively.

Health Education is treated as a distinct subject of study in teacher preparation programmes in our country, although the emphasis given on this subject varies in different universities. It is a specialized branch of knowledge and is the concern of the specialists. Teachers are not supposed to be experts in this field. But they are expected to possess working knowledge of health-related matters so as to be able to guide young boys and girls and the community members on health attitudes, habits, practices and even suggest ways and means to overcome general health problems.

We all need experiences which will influence our understanding, attitudes, habits and practices relating to the individual, family and community health. Doctors, nurses, teachers, health visitors and social welfare workers have important roles to play in educating people about matters relating to health. Although several formal and non-formal educational programmes relating to health matters have been conducted in schools, and many public campaigns have been launched through mass media and community meetings, yet glaring gaps exist between the required health standards and the existing state of health of our people. This book attempts to fill those gaps by orienting the prospective teachers towards the key aspects of health and physical education.

While writing this book, great care has been taken to present complicated facts in simple style and lucid manner. We hope that it will meet the needs of the readers.

We are grateful to Atlantic Publishers and Distributors (P) Ltd. for their valuable suggestions and publication of the book.

M. DASH
NEENA DASH

Contents

1

Health Education

1. THE CONCEPT OF HEALTH

A man's happiness in life depends upon good health, vigour and vitality. Half the pleasures of the world are denied to a person who is of ill-health. What is health? To some people 'health means a sound mind in a sound body.' A sound mind or a sound body develops only in a sound environment. Thus by 'health' we may mean 'a sound mind in a sound body in a sound environment.'

For ordinary medical purposes health includes:

(i) the growth and development of the body and its different organs in accordance with the standard norms from age to age;

(ii) the proper functioning of the various systems of the body;

(iii) proper vigour and energy to conduct one's daily activities;

(iv) freedom from disease and resistance to disease; and

(v) freedom from disabilities.

The World Health Organisation (WHO, 1948) defines health, as "a state of complete physical, mental and social well-being and not merely absence of disease or infirmity". Good health means the proper functioning of the physique (physical parts of the body), the chemique (chemical reactions inside the body), and the psychique (the harmonious functioning of the mind). Good health presupposes the existence of sound physical and social environments in which man lives.

2. MEANING OF HEALTH EDUCATION

In a modern community everybody needs to know and follow the rules of healthy living in order to keep well. We all need a good stock of basic general knowledge about healthful living and health services—a knowledge which can be readily applied at the right moment both in our private life and public life. We all need experiences which will influence our understanding, attitudes, habits and practices relating to the individual, family and community health. Doctors, nurses, teachers, health visitors, social welfare workers and even parents have important roles to play in educating people in general, and young children in particular about matters relating to health. Considered in this sense, "any educational programme in the school, formal or non-formal, or public campaign through mass media, pamphlets and community meetings and that deals with health matters may be termed as health education." In other words "health education refers to the totality of experiences from which individuals learn new behaviours (and probably change their old, conventional behaviours) related to their health habits and practices." Health education means "the process of providing or utilizing experiences for favourably influencing understandings, attitudes and practices relating to the individual, family and community health."

Health education is not a study of the human physiology and hygiene. It does not deal with the body or the physical state of the individual. It deals with physical as well as mental states of the individual. It deals with his body, mind and spirit. So health education is to be considered as a study of the good life intended to guide the individual moving from strength to strength in body, mind and spirit.

Health education can also be defined as education concerning the protection, preservation and promotion of health through self-care behaviour. It is a process of helping people identify their health problems, formulate their own objectives in the context of available resources and constraints and achieve these objectives with their own efforts. It should not aim merely at acquisition of all the latest knowledge in the field but should motivate the learner towards healthful living.

Health education has both a personal connotation and a

social significance. That is why we talk of personal health and community health. The individual must have proper understandings, attitudes and practices relating to health matters. But more important than this is the fact that every individual must have rational attitude towards the health of the community in which he lives. Recently community health is receiving greater attention from the health agencies than personal health. Thus health education should be understood not simply as the study of the good life of the individual but also as promoting and maintaining good community health. Health education is necessary for the individual as an individual. It is equally necessary for the individual as a member of the community. Health has a preventive side and remedial side. The preventive side is more important than the remedial side. Health education, at present, emphasizes the preventive and social aspects of health.

3. SCOPE OF HEALTH EDUCATION

Health education is a life-long process. It is not meant only for children at school or at home, it is meant for all boys and girls, children and adults, men and women, individuals and the community. An individual, as he passes from one stage to the other stage of his development, can profit from the experiences provided through health education from time to time. Health education is provided in an informal way by parents, in a formal way by the teachers, doctors, nurses and health workers and in a non-formal way in community centers.

It is not confined to the physical aspects of the individual's growth and development. It also deals with mental health of the individual. It is concerned with both personal and community health. It is concerned with both prevention and cure of diseases. In a broad sense, health education deals with national as well as international health standards and status. For example AIDS is both a national concern and an international concern. Thus the scope of health education is very wide. It includes a large number of fields like medicine, nursing, public health, nutrition, physiology and hygiene and safety education, etc. There are 13 broad areas of health education. Each area can be broken down into specific units, each unit having a number of divisions and sub-divisions. The 13 broad areas of health education are as follows:

(i) Care of all parts of the human body.

(ii) Prevention of diseases to all parts of the human body.

(iii) Non-remediable health conditions.

(This includes recognition, acceptance and availability of medical care for conditions caused by malfunctions or defects of the human body).

(iv) First-Aid/Red Cross.

(v) Safety education.

(This includes recognition and avoidance of hazards causing disability or death in modern living).

(vi) Mental health.

(vii) Nutrition education.

(This includes the science of nutrition, improvement of daily dietary habits to ensure wise selection and use of food).

(viii) Community health problems.

(This includes environmental sanitation and services of agencies promoting health).

(ix) Consumer health.

(This includes wise selection of health products and services and agencies concerned with the control of these products and services).

(x) Adult health education such as AIDS.

(xi) Family life education.

(xii) Misuse of alcohol, tobacco and other stimulants and depressants like *bhang*.

(xiii) International health.

4. OBJECTIVES OF HEALTH EDUCATION

The objectives of health education are inherent in its definition. Health education is the process of providing or utilizing experiences for favourably influencing understanding, attitudes and practices relating to individual, family, and community health. Thus health education aims at developing in children:

(i) Understanding of health concepts.

(ii) A rational attitude towards health situations—personal, family and community health matters.

(iii) Good health habits and practices.

In addition to the above three objectives, the following objectives are also important:

(i) Creating an awareness among people about their health status, health needs and requirements.

(ii) Developing among the people a continuing interest in health education.

(iii) Helping people appreciate and make use of health services.

(iv) Creating a healthful environment in the community.

The World Health Organisation has listed the aims of health education as follows:

(i) To ensure that health is valued as an asset in the community;

(ii) To equip the people with skills, knowledge and attitudes, to enable them to solve their health problems by their own actions and efforts; and

(iii) To promote the development and proper use of health services.

5. THE PROGRAMME OF HEALTH EDUCATION

Achievement of the objectives of health education is not an easy task. It is easy to chalk out programmes of health education which are, at times, very ambitious. But it is very difficult to implement the programmes in order that the objectives are achieved. The following few steps may be useful to health workers:

(i) Our people are guided by certain misbelieves, superstitions, stereotyped practices and unscientific ideas about health matters and habits. We have to impress upon them the evil effects of bad health habits and practices, convince them about the merits of scientific health habits and practices and motivate them to adopt good habits and practices as part of their daily living and growing up.

(ii) Mass media like newspaper, radio, television and short, documentary flims may be used to develop people's knowledge, understanding, attitudes and skills relating to health habits and practices.

(iii) Health instruction should form an integral part of the school curriculum at all stages to change the present unhealthy habits and practices of school going children and develop in them good health habits and practices.

(iv) Health education should also be considered as an integral part of all teacher education programmes so that the teachers equipped with such knowledge can guide students, parents, and other community members on matters of personal and community health.

(v) Health education will be successful in achieving its objectives only through coordinated efforts of various agencies and personnel-health agencies, community development agencies, educational institutions, mass media, community leaders and workers, teachers, doctors and other health workers.

6. PRINCIPLES OF HEALTH EDUCATION

First: Health education is concerned with everyday living as it affects the individual, his family, and his community. Health education deals not only with the health problems of the individual but also with those of the family and of the pupils within a classroom and school, and with those of the community and the nation as well.

Second: Health education deals with specific facts and not with general rules and statements. Health education is based on the results of experimentation, research and conclusions of various branches of science-medicine, dentistry, public-health, nursing, nutrition, pharmacy, etc. Paeudo information, misleading and ambiguous statements and disorganized and meaningless subject-matter have no place in health education.

Third: Health education is positive in its approach. Health education does not moralize or coerce but provides reliable factual evidence (e.g. relation between smoking and lung cancer) so that the individual can form positive opinions to guide his actions. Valid health information that is positive in its approach may be able to redirect a developing non-beneficial health behaviour into one that will be beneficial.

Fourth: Health education has a five-pronged attack. It attempts to improve the individual's physical and mental health status, erase the pseudo information, eliminate attitudes retarding improvement of his health status, promote health practices that benefit him, and stimulate continuous interest in health education.

Fifth: Health education depends on the teacher's (or instructor's) enthusiasm and interest. If the teacher or the instructor is disinterested and apathetic, health education has no opportunity to accomplish its purposes.

Sixth: Health education is based on objective information about the individual's physical and mental health status and his health practices, attitudes, interests and knowledge. It should be based on the individual's health needs and interests.

7. IMPORTANCE OF HEALTH EDUCATION FOR TEACHERS

Health education is a social responsibility. It is the business of the whole community and in particular of parents to see that the rising generation gets the best possible general training in matters of health. But parents cannot be expected to do everything single-handed. A strong professional team which includes doctors, health visitors and social welfare workers of every kind should be at work all the time to make sure that parents and children alike are living in as healthy an environment as possible and that help is available when needed. Within this team, the teacher's special relationship with young people at school provides him with a unique opportunity of giving them the training in matters of health which they need.

Any serious study of health education involves the training of teachers. The pattern of training reflects the general pattern of health education in the schools. Every teacher has a contribution to make and must be properly briefed. He must have at least a sound general knowledge of the main aspects of health education. He need not be an expert but he should know more than he has to pass on. Equally important, he must understand children when he is teaching, how they grow, how their minds work, what health means to them and how they can be introduced to it in such a way that they will still practise what they were taught even after leaving school. Finally he will, to a great extent, be teaching by personal example. To carry conviction in matters of health, he must himself practise what he is preaching. Knowledge, understanding of children, and a good example, all are necessary and the teacher training programme should be concerned with all three.

In teacher training programme, health education should be treated as a distinct and definite subject. It should be a compulsory subject for all students undergoing training to become teachers. The student should be helped to consider all that he leans about health in relation to the needs and nature of growing children. Knowledge about health habits and practices and understanding of children should form part of the course on health education. Theoretical knowledge should be coupled with small-group discussion and practical experiences such as observation of children, maintaining health records, visits to health centres, etc.

The actual contents of the course on health education vary from institution to institution within a country and even in different countries. This is, at times, desirable because the needs and requirements of children and the community vary from region to region and from country to country. However, certain components are common to all institutions. It is not necessary that every teacher should become an export in matters of health. It is necessary that every teacher must have essential knowledge about health matters. The following contents should, therefore, be included in a course on health education for teachers:

- Healthful School Environment.
- School Health Services.
- Health Education in Schools such as:
- Preventive measures for communicable diseases,
- Food and Nutrition.
- First Aid and Safety.
- Posture.
- Leisure, Play and Recreation.
- Physical Education Programme in Schools.
- Cleanliness.
- Care of the body.
- Yogasana.

Besides these contents, there are some other content areas which may be taught through other subjects prescribed for teacher education programme. For example, mental health and normal development at various stages of growth may be taught through a course on educational psychology.

In view of its importance, health education should be taught by health personnel in teacher training institutions. If an institution does not have health personnel, such as doctors and nurses, specially trained teacher educators should teach the subject to the teachers under training. It is unfortunate that health education is taught in training colleges and books are written by lecturers who had neither studied health education nor undergone training on health education.

Health education should not only be included in courses of study for pre-service teacher education programme but it must be given due importance in inservice teacher education programmes. Teachers who had never studied a course in health education should be selected and asked to attend short courses, seminars, conferences and various training programmes on health education.

Pre-service and in-service training of teachers on matters of health can contribute greatly in enabling teachers to guide children, parents and the community members to learn new behaviours relating to health habits and health practices. The National Policy of Education (1986) and the Programme of Action (Contents and Processes of Education) have given emphasis on teaching health and physical education in schools. The teacher education programme should be designed properly so that the recommendation of NPE, 1986 and the Programme of Action can be implemented effectively.

8. RESPONSIBILITIES OF THE HOME

The child's health is primarily a parental responsibility. Such responsibility does not end even after the child enters the school. Hence it is the home which has a major responsibility in educating children on matters of health:

(i) The first responsibility of the home is to teach desirable health knowledge, health attitude and health practices to the child and to break his undesirable health habits following the principles of conditioning.

(ii) Children learn a great deal of health behaviour through observation, modelling and imitation. Hence in teaching desirable health behaviour to children, the family members should show desirable health behaviour as a way of life so that young children can observe parental behaviour and imitate these behaviour patterns.

(iii) In teaching desirable health behaviours parents can make use of the following approaches:

- Verbal advice (incidential and intentional).
- Supplying health literature to the child according to his age.
- Watching TV programmes, listening to radio programmes and showing picture books.
- Health counseling as and when needed.
- Taking the child to the family doctor or the health centre for consultation, medical check-up and treatment.

In addition to the above, the home has the following responsibilities relating to the health of the child and family members:

(i) Parents must be willing to supply information concerning illness, injury, operation, possible health hazards, health habits and emotional health problems of family members.

(ii) Parents should develop close working relations with family doctors. This means interchange of health information among parents and doctors, seeking health guidance and carrying out the doctor's requests.

(iii) Parents should take the responsibility of correcting the child's health habits as reported by the school or the doctor.

(iv) They should cooperate with the school on matters relating to medical examination, immunization, etc.

(v) Parents should be present at medical examinations performed in the school or by the family doctors.

(vi) Parents should be aware of their limited information about health and become better informed about health matters.

(vii) Parents should seek early immunization of their child.

(viii) Parents should be vigilant about the personal hygiene of the family members and give advice to them as and when required.

(ix) The home should be a healthful environment for family members.

(x) The family members should participate in all health camps, health exhibitions and other programmes organised in the community.

(xi) They should participate actively in the prevention and control of communicable diseases.

(xii) Each member in the family should provide support to the needy, particularly young children and old ones in their illness, injury or accidents.

(xiii) There should be healthy social and emotional climate in the home and this will help to promote healthy mental health among members of the family.

9. RESPONSIBILITIES OF THE SCHOOL

Even though health education of the child is primarily the responsibility of the home, the school has a major responsibility in this regard. The school's responsibilities primarily centre around the following aspects:

(i) The school has to teach new behaviours, attitude and habits relating to health depending upon the age, experience, interests and abilities of students in different grades.

(ii) Sometimes children may forget health knowledge, health attitudes and health habits learned in the home and in earlier grades. The school's responsibility lies in reteaching those behaviours, attitudes and practices relating to health.

(iii) Sometimes the school may supplement the knowledge, attitudes and practices taught by parents in the home.

(iv) Children might have learned incorrect habits and unfavourable attitudes because of social, cultural and religious beliefs and faiths. The school's responsibility lies in correcting ineffective health habits and attitudes of children through discussion, understanding, rational thinking and self-decision making.

(v) Whether the school teaches, reteaches, supplements or corrects the health knowledge, attitudes and habits of students, teachers should take the help of the following methods and approaches:

- Lecture.
- Discussion.
- Demonstration.
- Audio-Visual aids.

- Visits to health centres, community sites, health camps and health exhibitions.
- Guest lecture by doctors.

(vi) The school should organise 'health day' or 'health weeks' from time to time to create awareness among students and parents about the importance of healthful living and the evil effects of ill-health.

(vii) Health appraisal, health examination and health services should form an integral part of the school's programme.

(viii) The school should work in close cooperation with the health department and health personnel.

(ix) The school should maintain health cards for each and every student regularly and continuously.

(x) The school should ensure a healthful living.

(xi) Health education should be provided through different subjects like General Science, Bio Science, Geography, Language and through Physical Education.

(xii) Teachers teaching about health should adopt health habits and health attitudes as a way of their life. Unless teachers possess scientific attitudes towards health related matters, unless they show healthy habits and unless they are knowledgeable on health matters they will not be successful in providing health education to students.

10. RESPONSIBILITIES OF THE COMMUNITY

In addition to the responsibilities of the home and the school, the community has a major role to play with regard to health education:

(i) The community should extend full cooperation to the health department and health personnel for organising health camps, health exhibitions, health survey and community health day.

(ii) Awareness programmes can be organised by community centre from time to time in collaboration with Panchayat Samiti.

(iii) Whenever any disease occurs in any family the entire community should be made alert to prevent and control the spread of the disease. The community members should come forward voluntarily to extend their cooperation and advice to the victimized family. Mutual cooperation and support among community members can promote community health.

(iv) The community centre should organise meetings, street plays, folk dance, folk music, etc., to convey the message of health education among the community members.

(v) Community cleanliness programmes (cleaning of ponds, road sites, village campus, etc.) should be organised from time to time to create awareness, develop favourable attitude and encourage health practices among community members relating to healthful living in the community.

(vi) The community centre should encourage all families for immunization of their children and other members whenever such facilities are made available in the community.

(vii) The community should create awareness among its members about the population situation in the community, help them understand the consequences of rapid population growth, develop in them a rational attitude towards population situation in their family, community, state and the nation and encourage them to take a decision relating to small family norm as a guarantee for a better health and quality of life of its members.

(viii) The community should strive to create a healthy socio-emotional climate among various families. Healthy social and emotional climate in families will lead to healthy climate in the community.

2

Health Education in Schools

1. WHAT IS SCHOOL HEALTH EDUCATION?

Health is a precious possession sought by everyone to make life fuller and richer. It is the business of the community to ensure that each individual maintains a healthy body and a healthy mind and leads a healthy life. So far as young children are concerned, adults take the responsibility of promoting the health of their children. More specifically, schools and their teachers have a significant role to play in this regard. The increasing number of illiterate parents, particularly in our country, the over-crowding of children in classrooms, hazards of modern-day living and a vast of other factors necessitate the organisation of school heath programme.

Health education in school refers to three inter-related programmes:

(a) Health Instruction to Students,

(b) Healthful School Living, and

(c) School Health Services.

Each of these three programmes is defined below:

Health Instruction to Students is defined as: The process of providing experiences to students for influencing their understandings, attitudes and skills relating to health habits and practices.

Healthful School Living is defined as: The utilisation of safe and wholesome environment, consideration of individual health, organising the school day, and planning classroom procedures to favourably influence the emotional, social and physical health.

School Health Services is defined as: The procedures used by physicians, dentists, nurses, teachers, etc. designed to appraise, protect and promote optimum health of students and school personnel.

School health education should not be regarded as a separate field of study or the work of a single teacher of health education. The scope of health education in school is so vast that it requires the concerted efforts of all school personnel for its implementation to foster the physical, mental and social well-being of children, parents and teachers.

2. SCOPE OF SCHOOL HEALTH EDUCATION

According to Williams and Brownwell (1956), the scope of school health education consists of three aspects viz.:

(a) Healthful School Living.

(b) Health Instructions.

(c) Health Services.

These three aspects have the general purpose of educating the child about health and hygiene:

(a) *Healthful School Living*: It deals with hygienic and sanitary aspects of school environment and organization, besides positive pupil-teacher relationship which are basic to a sound psychological and social health of children. Health of pupils reflects itself in aspects like work habits, cleanliness, emotional control, social relationship and clarity of thinking. Healthful school atmosphere can be created by improving the physical environment which includes lighting, ventilation, safe seating arrangements, cleanliness, water supply and so on; organizational elements like school schedules of rest and work, time-table, class size, examination schemes, etc. Pupil-teacher relationship shapes the discipline in the school and establishes the give and take process in every aspect of education, right from basic health to basic literacy.

(b) *Health Instruction*: It includes three stages *viz.*, acquainting the students with scientific facts and information conductive to healthy living, integration of this knowledge with actual life and guiding the children to transfer this living to the school, to the home and to the community. The success of health instruction depends to a large extent on the materials, means and personnel which help them to acquire health habits, skills and attitudes.

(c) *Health Services*: These have three functions, i.e., appraisal, remedial and protective. The appraisal functions include medical examinations for disease and defect. The protective functions include measures like first aid, vaccination, inoculations, etc. The remedial functions include not only corrective services but also follow-up services. All these experiences which the child is exposed to are educative in the sense that they help the child to live a healthy life.

3. HEALTH INSTRUCTION AT DIFFERENT STAGES

Health instruction is an essential aspect of health education is schools. It should be a regular feature of the daily life and work of the school. It should be provided through different school subjects and programmes particularly general science, physical education programme, language, geography and environmental study. As children pass from one stage to the next stage of education, or from one school to the other, continuity should be maintained in the teaching of health education. There are different stages of education and so also there are different stages of health education. Health education should vary from stage to stage in terms of its objectives, contents or learning experiences and methods of teaching:

Lower Primary Stage

***Objectives in the Cognitive Domain*:**

- To know and understand the external parts of the human body and their functions.
- To understand that adequate nutritious food is necessary for the growth of the body and maintenance of health.
- To understand the importance of cleanliness and sanitation of his surroundings.
- To understand the importance of taking care of different parts of the body.
- To recognise the common diseases prevalent in the

locality and understand their preventive and control measures including immunization.

- To establish relationship between nutritional intake in daily diet and nutritional disorders and deficiency diseases.
- To recognise the need and importance of personal cleanliness for healthful living.
- To develop elementary knowledge about first-aid and care of the sick at home.
- To learn the concept of safe water and develop the method or techniques of keeping the water safe.
- To develop an understanding of personal and community health practices such as proper toilet habits, disposal of garbage and disposal of waste water, etc.
- To understand the health needs, importance of rest, sleep, exercise, cleanliness and recreation for the maintenance of health.
- To identify various processes and techniques to be followed for the protection and care of various body parts.
- To understand that smoking and chewing tobacco is injurious to health.

Objectives in the Psycho-motor Domain

- To keep various parts of the body clean.
- To demonstrate to younger sibling, how to clean various parts of their body and clothes.
- To select and identify food items according to their nutritive value and to eat food in proper combinations from all major food groups.
- To participate in cleanliness campaigns in schools and community.
- To take necessary safety precautions in day to day life and take appropriate first-aid measures at the time of accidents and emergency.

- To provide proper care to sick and young children.
- To participate in food preparation, food serving and to follow proper food sanitation practices and avoid wastage of food.
- To demonstrate simple techniques of making of water safe for drinking.

Objectives in the Affective Domain

- To take interest in finding out how different external parts of the body function.
- To take interest in selecting and developing taste in eating food from different food groups and finding out what kinds of food are available in the locality.
- To appreciate the need of avoiding wastage of food at all levels.
- To appreciate the importance of physical, mental and social well being.
- To acquire a taste for the good and beautiful things in the environment and develop interest in finding out how the environment can be kept clean and beautiful.
- To appreciate the importance of drinking safe water.
- To appreciate the role of home, school, community and other agencies in promoting healthy living.
- To appreciate the importance of first-aid and care of the sick.
- To appreciate the harmful effects of smoking and chewing tobacco.

Content Areas/Learning Experiences

Based on the above objectives the learning opportunities in health education will be made available in the following content areas:

- External parts of human body-structure and functions.
- Care of external body parts.
- Personal cleanliness.

- Personal health practices.
- Food types, values and sources.
- Food consumption, desirable practices, avoiding wastage and spillage, etc.
- Environmental cleanliness and sanitation.
- Communicable diseases, causes, transmission, prevention and control.
- Accidents, first-aid and care of the sick.
- Harmful effects of smoking or chewing tobacco, consuming alcohol, etc.

Upper Primary Stage

Objectives in the Cognitive Domain

- To explain and discuss various organ systems and functions of body including the process of reproduction.
- To understand the concept of nutrients, their value in daily diet and to select appropriate food items in order to prepare a balanced diet.
- To explain the causes of deficiency diseases and establish their relationship with deficiency.
- To learn about various techniques and procedures of food preservation and storages and rules of food sanitation.
- To discriminate and distinguish between safe and unsafe water and learn the ways of purifying water.
- To explain the process of how communicable diseases spread and the measures taken for their prevention.
- To discuss the growth and development characteristics and find out contrast in growth patterns between boys and girls.
- To identify personal and community health practices conducive for healthy environment in the home, community and village.
- To recognise ill-effects of tobacco, drugs and narcotics on health.

Objectives in the Psycho-motor Domain

- To develop skills of taking care of eyes, ear, teeth, and genital part of body.
- To demonstrate safety and first aid measures during accidents and emergencies.
- To provide essential care to the sick at home.
- To participate in environmental sanitation in home, school and locality.
- To demonstrate procedures and techniques of purifying water for drinking.
- To observe socially accepted norms of behaviour in day-to-day life.

Objectives in the Affective Domain

- To imbibe regular health habits of keeping body parts clean.
- To develop positive attitude towards observance of health rules in schools and the community.
- To develop the habit of consulting health personnel in the state of sickness and not to take to self-medication.
- To develop regular habits of washing hands before taking food, not wasting food and cleaning eating place before and after food.
- To inculcate regular habits of taking food at regular time and in adequate quantity.

Content Areas

To achieve the objectives of this stage the learning opportunities can be wcven around the following major areas:

- Internal organisations of the human body and the functioning of different systems with special reference to reproduction.
- Nutrients, food groups, balanced diet—its concepts, deficiency, diseases and disorders, food preservation and food sanitation.

- Concept of safe water, precautions necessary for keeping water safe.
- What is disease—how it spreads, differences between communicable and non-communicable diseases—their causes, symptoms and preventive measures.
- Desirable personal and community health practices for the prevention of communicable diseases.
- Meaning of growth and development, characteristics of growth in boys and girls—physical, mental, social, and environmental, facilities conducive for growth/and development.
- General principles, procedures of first-aid, safety and home nursing.
- Harmful effects of tobacco, drugs and narcotics on health.

Methods of Instruction

The effectiveness of learning experiences to achieve the objectives depends upon the methods and materials of health instruction adopted by the teacher of health instruction. There is no specific or single method of instruction which can be effectively used for all areas of health instruction. Moreover health instruction is to be considered as a cooperative responsibility involving the work of parents, teachers and professional people. So the teacher should not be regarded as the only person responsible for health instruction to students. But he has a major role to play in this regard.

The teacher is the real health guide for the students. Even in underprivileged and underdeveloped communities people look for the advice of the teacher on health matters. Thus the teacher must have good knowledge and understandings about health maters. What is more important is the fact that the teacher must be an example for the students, he must practise everything in his daily life what he intends to preach. For example, a teacher who smokes or takes "Khaini" cannot be effective in preaching about the harmful effects of smoking or taking "Khaini".

In classrooms, health instruction must be based upon the needs, interests and receptive powers of students. Appraisal of health status of students should be the starting point of health instruction. Health appraisal of students on the basis of medical examination by doctors and health records will indicate the health status, needs and interests of students. The principles of health education which we discussed earlier should be the guidelines of providing health instruction to students. In addition to these, teacher's visit to the home of a student can provide information about the health problem of the student and this will help in giving the needed instruction about health matters.

In the elementary schools direct instruction is found more effective than incidental learning. The teacher can make use of the following methods for providing health instruction:

- Discussion method.
- Question-answer method.
- Problem-solving method.
- Dramatization.
- Demonstration.
- Narration.
- Field trips.
- Story telling.
- Child-to-child method.
- Lecture by a medical officer, nurse or some other invited speakers.

Much of the teacher's work can be simplified if he can function in collaboration with the health department and health personnel and if he can encourage children to watch television for special programmes and advices on health matters. Various visual materials like slides, pamphlets, pictures, charts, diagrams and booklets can be used for health instruction purposes.

How much time should be allotted to health education in the elementary schools? For many years, educators and physicians have recommended that health education be allotted the same amount of time as that given to other major fields of learning.

To strengthen health and safety practices that are fundamental to the child's well-bring now and in the future, health education must be given as much time for its content as other subjects have been given. The success of health instruction depends upon the time and resources available, and the interest and enthusiasm of the teacher. Health instruction should be an integral part of the elementary school curriculum.

Secondary Stage

Health instruction in secondary schools should be a continuation of all that has gone before. The following objectives, contents and methods of teaching are suitable for health instruction in secondary schools:

Objectives of Teaching Health Education

The objectives of teaching health education in secondary schools can be discussed under three heads:

- cognitive area (health knowledge);
- affective area (heath attitude);
- psycho-motor area (health habits and practices).

Objective relating to Health Knowledge

The objectives of health education in schools should be to help students:

(i) To identify different nutrients and their functions.

(ii) To understand the quantity and proportion of various nutrients in the food to make a balanced diet.

(iii) To understand the concept of malnutrition and under-nutrition, their harmful effects on health, and the measures to prevent and control them.

(iv) To identify the causes, symptoms and mode of transmission of communicable diseases, their preventive and remedial measures.

(v) To establish relationship between individual health and community health.

(vi) To identify community health problems and establish their relationships with population growth.

(vii) To identify socio-cultural values and to establish their relationship with heath practices.

Objectives relating to Health Attitudes

(i) To develop positive attitude towards observance of health rules in their life.

(ii) To realize the importance of timely immunization for child survival.

(iii) To develop a rational attitude towards small family norm as an essential component to quality of life.

(iv) To develop a scientific attitude towards social and cultural values and beliefs relating to health practices in the community.

(v) To develop a positive attitude for taking responsibility for his own health and giving support to others during their ill-health.

Objectives relating to Health Practices

(i) To adopt proper food habits.

(ii) To develop good habits of healthful living.

(iii) To take the benefits of medical services at the time of ill-health.

(iv) To select locally available food items (cheaper food at low cost) to ensure balanced diet.

(v) To avoid taking food outside under unhygienic conditions.

(vi) To adopt measures for ensuring personal hygiene and community health.

(vii) To provide first-aid to the injured in the family, school and community.

(viii) To follow safety measures on the road, in the home and in the school (classroom, playground, laboratories).

(ix) To avoid taking tobacco, chewing betel, smoking and drugs.

(x) To participate in the public health campaigns, and community cleanliness programme.

(xi) To participate and help people at the time of epidemics and natural calamities.

Contents/Learning Experiences in Different Subjects

In order to achieve the above stated objectives of health education, certain contents or learning experiences should be provided through different subjects. Usually such contents are provided through Language, General Science, Biological Science, Geography, Health and Hygiene, Home Science and Physical Education. Certain contents can be provided through specific subjects. For example, contents relating to food and nutrition can be provided through General Science. Certain contents can be provided through a number of subjects. For example, facts relating to population growth and population problems can be provided through Language, Geography and General Science. The following contents should be provided through these subjects:

- Personal and community health practices and their bearing on the health status of the individual and the community.
- Communicable, non-communicable, and deficiency diseases—their causes, symptoms, remedial and preventive measures.
- Food and nutrition, balanced diet.
- Population growth, consequences and implications for individual and family health, small family norm.
- Child survival measures—immunization, growth monitoring, breast feeding, food supplements, birth spacing and family life education.
- Principles of safe motherhood, age of marriage, health risks with frequent pregnancy.
- Socio-cultural beliefs and values conducive to health promotion.
- Harmful effects of tobacco, drug, smoking, etc.
- AIDS.
- First-aid and safety.
- Games and sports, yoga.

Methods of Teaching

Health education can be provided directly or incidentally through various subjects. It should be based on the needs, interest and receptive ability of students. It should not be the sole responsibility of any single teacher. It should depend upon the cooperative efforts of teachers, doctors, nurses and parents. The success of health education depends on how much time the teacher devotes and how sincerely he works for promotion of health of his pupils.

In developing health knowledge, health attitude and health practices of students the teacher can make use of the following methods and techniques:

- Discussion.
- Lecture.
- Problem-solving.
- Demonstration.
- Field Trips.
- Community survey.
- Medical examination.
- Maintenance of health records.
- Verbal reports.
- Guest lecture by specialists.
- Private or personal counseling by lady doctors.
- Audio-visual aids.

4. CREATING A HEALTHFUL ENVIRONMENT IN SCHOOLS

Healthful school living is an important aspect of school health programme. It includes environmental factors, school nutritions, community resources, health of the school personnel and school day. The school personnel and pupils have definite functions in maintaining healthful school living. In this section we shall discuss some steps for creating a healthful environment in the school.

Healthful environment in the school refers to such factors as improving the school building, water supply, sewage and garage disposal, heating and ventilation, lighting, and school furniture:

(a) *The School Building*: The school building plays a very crucial role in creating a healthful environment in the school. In our country, schools function in various types of buildings, pucca, partly pucca, kacha, thatched houses and tents or temporary sheds. There are also schools which function in the open air. In whatever type of building the school may function, it contributes greatly in maintaining a healthful environment for the pupils and the teacher.

The school building must be located in a place away from the hustle and bustle of the town or the village. The site must be such that water does not accumulate or form mud during the rainy season. So the school building must be situated on a high land. The building must not face east or west directly so that it has maximum Sun in winter and minimum of Sun in summer. It must be located in a place where free and pure air is available in plenty. We shall discuss light and ventilation in detail later in this section. For purpose of light and ventilation and other conveniences the building should be constructed with approved plan either as **E** type or **H** type or **C** type.

A minimum of 5 acres of land should be made available for a primary school. In case of middle schools and secondary schools the requirements are 7 acres and 10 acres of land respectively. The number of rooms, the purpose of rooms, the size of the room, playground and other facilities depend upon the land available for the purpose.

(b) *Water Supply*: A school building utilizes water in many ways. In every instance, water must be purified and not polluted. Polluted water can be the source of such waterborne diseases as typhoid, fever, bacillary dysentery, cholera, and amebic dysentery. To provide water supply free from pollution, the supply must be obtained from a public water system or tube-well.

The most common use of water in a school is for satisfying thirst. A minimum of one drinking fountain for each 100 pupils and one fountain on each floor is desirable. The most satisfactory type of fountain does not allow the mouth of the student to come in contact with the nozzle and the waste water to fall on the nozzle. As part of health instruction, teachers of the primary grades can show children how to use drinking fountains. Facilities for washing hands and feet after lunch and play should be available and such habits should be cultivated from the very beginning of primary education. Water should also be supplied for toilet rooms and washbasins. When water for drinking and washing purposes is supplied from sources other than the public water system care must be taken to see that what we supply is pure water and not polluted water.

(c) *Sewage and Garbage Disposal*: The housefly and common house mouse will be found in elementary and secondary schools that have improper sewage and garbage disposal. The housefly can carry the causative agents of typhoid fever and other intestinal infections in addition to diseases caused by bacteria and some viruses. The common house mouse can be the reservoir for the infective agents of typhus fever, rat bite fever and some other diseases.

Sewage includes the waste water from washbasins, toilet facilities, drinking fountains, and lavatories. It includes surface drainage water and human body wastes. When there is improper sewage disposal, diseases such as typhoid, fever, cholera, dysenteries, hookworm and other intestinal infections may result.

Waste is identified as waste paper from classroom and rubbish. A breeding place for flies and other insects is created when there is improperly disposed waste. Garbage includes the waste animal and vegetable material from kitchen or canteen. Improper disposal of garbage becomes a breeding place for flies and other insects and feeds rats and stray animals.

Sewage should be discharged into a public sewer system or a private or institutional type sewer system. All waste should be placed in galvanized iron cans with tight fitting covers, and should be separated from garbage. Waste may be collected by the municipality or burned daily. Garbage should be placed in a galvanized iron can with a tight-fitting cover and separated from waste. Garbage from a school building should be collected daily. Garbage can should be cleaned, disinfected and dried each time they are emptied. Garbage should be collected by the municipality and disposed at a place for away from the town.

(d) *Ventilation*: Ventilation or distribution and movement of air in the school building is very important for healthful living. Fatigue signs appearing in students in the mid morning and mid after-noons may be caused by inadequate ventilation or inefficient system of ventilation. The teacher may feel comfortable and have a sense of well-being, but the student may be too warm or cold, seated in a draft, nauseated from classroom odors.

The teacher should see that fresh outdoor air is introduced into the air system of a school building so that a basic minimum quantity of air in cubic feet is provided per person, and body odors are removed. In order to ensure cross- ventilation the doors and windows must face each other in a south to north direction. In order to prevent polluted air moving into the classrooms the school building must be located in place away from the industrial plants, burning ghats, cremation grounds, dirty ponds and market place. Availability of fresh and pure air in the classroom reduces the possibility of infectious diseases spreading from pupil to pupil. Outdoor activities provide students fresh and pure air which they may not get in indoor activities. If the school has a pucca building and if funds permit ventilators may be provided in each and every classrooms.

(e) *Lighting*: A high quality of lighting and an adequate level of illumination are necessary for efficient performance of visual tasks. The teacher must see that the quality of illumination, the level of illumination, the reflections, the sun light or the electric lighting are all controlled so that they do not cause discomfort, distraction or invisibility but promote eye health. The doors and windows must be fixed in such a way that natural light passes into the classroom. When natural light is poor due to weather conditions or some other factors, artificial lighting arrangements should be made in the classroom. In any case the seating arrangement or furniture, teacher's position in the classroom, the walls, floor and the ceiling should be considered to ensure proper lighting and illumination and prevent reflection causing eye strain, discomfort or lack of visibility. Students should not sea facing the windows or the doors which allow bright light to come in or reflect directly. It is desirable to allow light from a side rather than directly from the front or the back. Students with visual difficulties should be placed in classroom positions that give them the best light in accordance with their individual visual difficulties. The windows must remain unshaded and open and window sills should be kept free form objects. All wall charts and maps that have become faded, dirty or worn should be eliminated from the classroom. The chalkboard should be clean and free from accumulating chalk dust. All board writings should be clear, large and consistent. The teacher should sit or stand in position directing students' vision away from the windows. Students should be allowed to change their seats when they desire more or less light.

(f) *School Furniture*: Many types of furniture are utilized for various classroom purposes. Among these the most common furniture are almirah, cup board, table, chairs, desks, blackboard, etc. For use by students long desk-bench combinations, individual desk-chair combinations, and individual low desk may be found in the classrooms. Individual desk-chair combination is always the best.

Desks and chairs should have a variety of designs and sizes, be movable and adjustable. No single designed piece of desk or chair is applicable to every teaching environment, nor can desk-chair combination of the same size be used at all grade levels.

Desks and chairs should be movable. Noiseless gliders placed on the legs will permit movement without the minimum of noise. The desks and chairs should be finished with light colours and these must be of light weight. Thus the students can push the desk-chair combination into different seating arrangements to improve the quality of light on the surface.

5. IMPORTANT CONCERNS AND ISSUES

Health is one of the most crucial indicators of individual progress and national development. Health, therefore, should be understood as both individual and national concern. In view of this, the status given to health education in the school curriculum assumes a great significance.

Since independence, considerable progress has been achieved in promotion of the health status of our people. Death rate has been reduced. The life expectancy at birth has risen from 32.7 years to over 54 years. (Health information of India: CBHIDGHS, Ministry of Health and Family Welfare, New Delhi, 1987). Inspite of this significant achievement, the health scenario in the country appears to be a cause of serious concern. This is mainly because the high increasing pressure of population growth continues to exert an adverse effect on the health status of our people. Inspite of considerable achievements in this area, infant mortality at present is around 104 (1984) per thousand live births. Only 31 per cent of our rural population has access to potable water supply, and 0.5% population enjoys basic facilities in sanitation (National Health Policy, 1983). The current level of achievement as well as broad indicators of achievement of certain basic health and family welfare goals which have been set out in the National Health Policy appear to be quite ambitious and therefore demand concerted efforts to achieve them. Needless to mention, this demands a bold health education policy and its vigorous implementation at all levels of education.

In order to achieve the goals set out for Health for All, it is imperative that our young children should acquire knowledge, skills and attitudes which will shape their health and have positive impact on their life style and thereby play a vital role in improving the health status of their community and nation at large.

Emphasising the importance of the School Health Programme, the National Health Policy has recommended that "Organised school health services integrally linked with the general, preventive and curative services would require to be established within a time limited programme".

The policy further states "The recommended efforts on various fronts would bear marginal results unless nation wide health education programmes, backed by appropriate communication strategy are launched to provide health information in easily understandable form to motivate the development of attitude for healthy living. The public health education programmes should be supplemented by health, nutrition and population education programmes in all educational institutions at various levels. Simultaneously efforts would require to be made to promote universal education especially adult and family education without which the various efforts to organise preventive and promotive health activities, family planning and improved maternal and child health cannot bear fruit."

The National Policy of Education (1986), has emphasised the need for the overall development of the young child. It states, "Recognising the holistic nature of child development, *viz.* nutrition, health and social, mental, physical, moral and emotional development, Early Childhood Care and Education (ECCE) will receive high priority and be suitably integrated with the Integrated Child Development Services Programme, wherever possible." The policy further states, "A full integration of child care and pre-primary education will be brought about, both as a feeder and a strengthening factor for primary education and for human resource development in general. In continuation of this stage the School Health Programme will be strengthened."

The section on Vocational Education in the Education Policy (1986), also stresses the development of appropriate categories of health worker. It states — "Health planning and health service management should optimally interlock with the education and training of appropriate categories of health manpower through health related vocational courses. Health education at the primary and middle level will ensure the commitment of the individual to family and community health, and leads to health related vocational courses at the +2 stage of higher secondary education."

It is heartening to note that the national intentions in both the policies are complementary and need to be judiciously integrated in the programmes of actions to attain the major goals.

Concerns

Social Concerns: Vast number of the children of school going age are not attending school. But whether these children are in school or not, they are learning about health every day. These children are developing values, attitudes, knowledge and skills from their parents, siblings, peer groups and other sources which will shape their health for life time. Some of these learnings are desirable and some are undesirable. Direct and indirect media of communication are also having great influence in shaping their behaviour. These attitudes and values of today's young people will determine the health of the community and nation as they will grow up to be future parents and leaders of the community. To achieve "Health for All", it is of paramount importance that they should be empowered to manage their health so as to enhance their quality of life and, in turn, the quality of the nation's future.

Pedagogical Concerns: For successfully influencing the health learning of young children, it is essential to have commitment and effective development of many resources. Strengthening of health education for school age children goes beyond the refinement and widespread application of existing methodology as well as developing some new methodology. While doing so it is necessary to take into account the diverse social, cultural and physical environment of the children. It also involves looking at children, how they learn and what influences their beliefs. Health cannot be separated from the total development of the individual. A positive health makes that development attainable whereas absence of such health imposes heavy restriction on it. Children must be made to realize that health is a high priority asset and they themselves are instrumental in affecting positive health, inspite of major cultural, social and economic constraints. For example, simple health practices of personal hygiene and environmental sanitation can go a long way in enhancing the quality of their life, and these practices are possible even in poor economic surroundings. The emphasis of health education in the school curriculum should be directed to this end.

Some of the important questions and issues that arise for proper implementation of health education programme in school are as under:

Issues

(i) What is the most effective way to integrate health education in the total school programme? Should it be:

- an independent subject to be taught by a subject teacher?
- integrated with other subjects?
- a part of management of physical, mental, emotional and social environment in school?
- a part of school health-services?
- pervasive to total school programme?

(ii) How much time should be allotted to health education transaction out of the time allocated at different levels in the National Curriculum for Primary and Secondary Education and National Curriculum for Higher Secondary Education?

(iii) How can more effective links be established among schools, families and other agencies of communities including the mass-media to minimise conflicts in value systems and maximize positive health learning?

(iv) How can long-sought, but rarely found effective coordination of efforts between the health and education sectors be achieved at national, state, district and local levels in areas such as:

- curriculum planning/revision/transaction;
- preparation of instructional materials;
- preparation of educational personnel through preservice and inservice education;
- improvement of school environment;
- health appraisal, referral and follow-up of students;
- enlisting community participation and participation of students in community-based health programmes; and
- monitoring and evaluation?

(v) To what extent can already overburdened teachers teaching other subjects be reasonably expected to shoulder responsibilities of health education transaction, observing and screening students for defects and deviations from normal health and maintaining health records?

(vi) How can teachers, lacking expertise and training in transaction and evaluation of health education be prepared to deal with the subject competently and confidently?

(vii) What should be the strategy of preparing health education faculty for teacher education institutions, health education planners and administrators for national, state and district level health education and educational institutions?

(viii) What strategy will be most effective for health education transaction for out of school children?

(ix) What will be the most effective mechanism to monitor health education transaction and environmental facilities in school for healthful living?

All these issues need to be talked for the successful implementation of the health education policy.

3

Physical Education

1. WHAT IS PHYSICAL EDUCATION?

For success in any field of human endeavour, the development and maintenance of a strong body and a healthy mind becomes an indispensable requirement. Earlier it was believed that the development and maintenance of a healthy mind could be made possible through the study of academic subjects like language, mathematics, science, social studies, etc. Physical education was considered to develop the body and to maintain it. It was defined as the education of the body or education of the physical. The concept of physical education as the education of the physical is no longer accepted today. It is now believed that the mind and the body are inseparable and that they function as integral part of our functioning as individuals. A sound mind exists in a sound body and a sound body presupposes a sound mind. Thus physical education is now considered as "education through the physical activities of the individual."

Physical education is an integral part of the total education process—a sub-system of general education—which enhances and integrates the physical, social and psychological aspects of an individual's life through direct physical activity. The main underlying idea is that physical education is education through the physical and of the physical. In this sense physical activities become real life experiences in educating the child physically, mentally and morally. These qualities like sportsmanship, obedience, team spirit, co-operative effort, loyalty and readiness to serve can be acquired through the education of the physical.

It is worthwhile to quote some of the definitions of physical education here.

"Physical education is the sum of those experiences which come to the individual through movement." (Delibert Obertuffer, 1970).

"Physical education is the sum of man's physical activities as to kind and conducted as to outcomes." (J.F. Williams, 1966).

"Physical education is an integral part of the total education process and as its aim, the development of physically, mentally, emotionally and socially fit citizens through the medium of physical activities which have been selected with a view to realizing these outcomes" (Charles E. Bucher, 1972).

In the contemporary school, physical education will be of great value for the general education of the child, nourishing his vitality and confidence and helping to develop him as a unified individual, with body, mind and spirit in time with each other. The modern concept of physical education includes not only training in the old sense but also the widest possible variety of experiences, including gymnastics, mountaineering, hiking, camping, yogasans, etc. Such forms of activity can make a profound appeal and it is sometimes hard to tell where the physical ends and the intellectual or the social, or the moral begins.

2. IMPORTANCE OF PHYSICAL EDUCATION

Physical education in schools was earlier considered to be an extra curricular activity and was pushed to the back seats, whereas now it is accepted as a curricular activity.

One of the tragic aspects of our general education is that a large majority of our school and college students have problems like poor health, postural defects, feet defects, overweight or underweight, defective sense organs, etc. Who or what is to be blamed—our homes, our civilization or our educational system? This indicates a need for serious rethinking into the scope of education and the necessity for redefining the scope, objectives, and means of educational development. Physical education comes as an appropriate sub-system of our educational system and tries to offer practical hints for wholesome development.

Education has to take the responsibility of all around development in the child by means of physical activity, and the teacher has to make use of various exercises to develop and maintain a physically fit body, psychologically sound mind and socially desirable outlook in the child. Most of the attitudes, skills and experience learned through physical education could be easily transferred to general education and finally to life. Physical education has become an integral part of general education and also a means of achieving all around development.

If physical education and its allied fields like yoga and gymnastics are to meet the demands of the society and take its due place in the scheme of general education then we must stop thinking merely in terms of competitions and tournaments, medals and prizes. Physical education should not end with routine activities like drill, games and sports because activities are not the end, they are only the means to achieve the end of all-around development in the student. In other words physical education is a tool in the scheme of general education and an integral part of total education.

The importance of physical education in the scheme of general education is evident from the following facts:

(i) Education involves the whole individual and physical education is a phase of general education.

(ii) Physical education activity is conducive to growth and development.

(iii) Physical education contributes to the constructive use of leisure.

(iv) Physical education provides for leadership training and training of emotions.

(v) Physical education provides opportunity for expression and creativity.

(vi) Physical education provides for overall development—intellectual development, spiritual development, personality development, and character development.

(vii) Physical education provides for organic development, and physical fitness.

(viii) Physical education develops neuro-muscular skills and habits of health and safety.

(ix) Physical education develops the whole man.

Recognising the importance of physical education in school the Secondary Education Commission (1952–54) said:

> "Unless physical education is accepted as an integral part of education and the education authorities recognise its need in all schools, the youth of the country which form its most valuable assets will never be able to pull their full weight in national welfare."

The Indian Education Commission (1964–66) emphasised the importance of physical education in the following words:

> "It must be emphasized that such education contributes not only to physical fitness but also to physical efficiency, mental alertness and the development of certain qualities like perseverance, team spirit, leadership, obedience to rules, moderation in victory and balance in defeat."

The National Policy of Education (1986) has recommended: "Sports and physical education are an integral part of the learning process, and will be included in the evaluation of performance. A nation-wide infrastructure for physical education, sports and games will be built into the educational edifice. The infrastructure will consist of playfields, equipment, coaches and teachers of physical education as part of the school improvement programme. Available open spaces in urban areas will be reserved for playgrounds, if necessary by legislation. Efforts will be made to establish sports institutions and hostels where specialised attention will be given to sports activities and sports related studies alongwith normal education. Appropriate encouragement will be given to those talented in sports and games. Due stress will be laid on indigenous traditional games. As a system which promotes an integrated development of body and mind Yoga will receive special attention. Efforts will be made to introduce Yoga in all schools, and to this end, it will be introduced in teacher training courses."

3. AIMS OF PHYSICAL EDUCATION

The field of physical education is characterized by the functions and objectives for which it exists. The scope of modern physical education programme is so broad that various authorities have listed various aims of physical education. For example, Clarke (1969), lists three aims of physical education:

(i) Physical fitness;

(ii) Social efficiency;

(iii) Culture.

Cowell and Schehn classify the aims into six groups:

(i) Development of organic power.

(ii) Development of the ability to maintain adaptive efforts.

(iii) Neuro-muscular development.

(iv) Personal and social adjustment.

(v) Intellectual development.

(vi) Emotional responsiveness.

Nash (1931), had also similar views about the aims of physical education. According to him the four developmental aims of physical education are:

(i) Organic development.

(ii) Neuro-muscular development.

(iii) Interpretive development.

(iv) Emotional development.

Wood and Cassidy (1934), listed two general aims and certain specific objectives:

General Aims

(i) Harmonious development during childhood which includes interest, capacities and abilities.

(ii) Harmonious development for useful adult life which includes interests, ideals and habits.

Specific Objectives

(i) Muscular growth.

(ii) Organic vigour.

(iii) Nervous vitality.
(iv) Good health habits.
(v) Correction of defects.
(vi) Good health service.
(vii) Supervision of mental hygiene.

Book Walter has given a concise and all-inclusive statement of the aim of physical education. "The aim of physical education is the optimum development of physically, socially and mentally integrated and adjusted individual through guided instruction and participation in selected total body sports, rhythmic and gymnasitc activities conducted according to social and hygienic standards."

The National Curriculum for Primary and Secondary Education—A framework (NCERT, 1985) contains the aims of physical education in a rather more concise form as follows: "Physical education in school should aim at development of health, strength and fitness of the body."

4. MINIMUM LEVELS OF LEARNING IN PHYSICAL EDUCATION

Students learn various subjects in the school. But the quality of education given in the secondary schools of our state is very poor. There is, at present, disparity in the quality of education given in the urban schools and rural schools, government schools and private schools. To reduce this disparity we have to ensure that all students passing a particular class or stage of education must have attained the minimum standard in respect of various subjects. The need to lay down Minimum Levels of Learning (MLL) emerges from the basic concern that irrespective of caste, creed, location, or sex, all students must be given access to education of a comparable standard. The major focus of the MLL policy is upon equity and reduction of existing disparities.

Minimum Levels of Learning (MLL) have been identified in Language, Mathematics, and Environmental Studies at the primary stage. MLL in respect of other subjects such as physical education, work experience and art and aesthetic education have not yet been identified. It has been decided to identify

MLL in those subjects in future. No attempt has yet been made to identify MLL in respect of various subjects at the secondary stage. MLL in respect of various subjects at the secondary stage will be identified only after successful experimentation with MLL at the primary stage.

Steps and strategies for identifying and promoting MLL in Physical Education:

(i) Learning a subject means acquiring certain competencies relating to that subject and having mastery over those competencies. For example learning a language at the primary stage means acquiring the basic language skills—listening, speaking, reading and writing upto a mastery level. The competencies to be acquired in physical activities may correspond to expected learning outcomes, or terminal behaviours or objectives of instruction in physical education. It is expected that after successfully participating in physical education activities the students will be able to:

- explore, experience and interact with their physical and social surroundings.
- realize the values of regularity, punctuality, cleanliness, industriousness, diligence, sense of duty and service, equality, co-operation, sense of responsibility, truthfulness, sense of achievement and national identity.
- develop as healthy, strong and physically fit individuals.

Minimum levels of learning in physical education can be stated in terms of these terminal competencies.

(ii) Once the terminal competencies are stated these competencies are broken down into sub-competencies. In other words each terminal competency is broken into sub-competencies. These sub-competencies are arranged in a hierarchical way or sequentially so that one sub-competency is related to the other sub-competency.

Acquisition of one sub-competency will help in acquiring the next sub-competency in the hierarchy.

(iii) The competencies and the sub-competencies are arranged sequentially from simple to complex and according to the maturity level of the learner in different classes.

(iv) Acquiring the competencies and/or sub-competencies relating to a particular class is the minimum level of learning in that class. Acquisition of all the competencies means mastery over the subject.

(v) It must be remembered that the MLL should be identified on the basis of their achievability, evaluability and continuity.

(vi) Once the MLL have been identified the next step is to select activities which will provide the required experiences to the students so that they will be able to attain the MLL in physical education. The physical activities should be selected according to age, interest, and ability of students, facilities available in the school for organisation of such activities, experience and expertise of the PET, and the funds available in the school for the purpose.

(vii) The next step is to supply the teacher's handbook on physical education to the PET. The handbook will be a guide for the PET to proceed systematically in promoting the MLL among the students of secondary schools.

(viii) One important strategy in promoting MLL among students is to equip the PET with the latest knowledge and skills in physical education. The PET should be deputed to participate in orientation programmes, refresher courses and short-term training programmes on MLL. Since the concept of MLL in physical education is new emphasis should be given on the training of PET, without which no PET will be able to promote MLL among students.

(ix) Steps and strategies I to VIII refer to the planning and preparation aspect. Implementation of the above strategy to promote MLL among students is very important. The teacher should organise and teach various physical activities in a carefully planned, systematic and step by step manner. The following activities may be organised in the school for promoting MLL among the students:

- Callisthenics;
- Gymnastics;
- Swimming;
- Yogasanas;
- Track and field events;
- Major games;
- Adventerous sports;
- Intramural competitions;
- Annual athletic meet, etc.

(x) Students should be encouraged to participate in these activities according to their interest and ability.

(xi) In teaching various games the teacher should follow the following techniques:

- Instruction about the various aspects of the game and the rules governing the games.
- Demonstration of various skills, sub-skills, etc., one by one.
- Practice by students relating to various skills sub-skills, etc., one by one.
- Combining all the skills and playing the game.
- Evaluation of their performance in respect of various skills and sub-skills.
- The teacher should give feedback to students regularly during practice and performance.
- The teacher should follow whole-part-whole method in teaching various skills.

(xii) Evaluation of students' progress in attaining the MLL is a very essential step. Formative evaluation and summative evaluation should be conducted by the PET relating to the MLL in physical education.

5. ORGANISATION OF PHYSICAL EDUCATION PROGRAMMES

Physical education is considered as an integral part of school education. As an integral part of general education it must occupy its due place in the school curriculum. In past, physical education was considered as an extra-curricular activity. In some schools physical education was not at all organised. Very few schools used to appoint PET. Even parents used to discourage their children for participation in physical education activities. Some parents used to consider these activities as mere waste of time and energy and detrimental to any academic progress. The situation in most schools has improved at present. Parents are now taking interest and encouraging their children for active participation in such activities.

If physical education is to achieve its aims it must be planned sensively and organised systematically.

(i) *Availability of Play Fields*: At present a large number of schools do not have play fields. As per the findings of the 5th All India Education Survey, out of 3955 secondary schools in Orissa only 2253 schools have playground facilities in usable conditions; 1149 schools have playground but not in usable conditions. If physical education is to be organised successfully the schools should have play fields in usable conditions. The playground should be clearly marked, lined and properly maintained. It must be kept neat and clean always.

(ii) *Provision of Games and Sports Equipment*: A successful programme of physical education depends on provision of games and sports equipment for students. At present many schools do not have games and equipment and few schools have limited equipment. State governments are supplying games and sports equipments to all the schools in a phased manner. In addition the department of sports also provide sports equipment to schools. The school can collect games fee from every student at the time of admission. The fees collected from the students can be utilized to purchase equipment for the school.

(iii) *The School Time Table*: The playfield is ready, games and sports equipment have been purchased. Now provision should be made in the school time-table for physical education activities. The National Curriculum for Primary and Secondary Education prepared by NCERT suggests the following allocation of time in school education for physical and health education:

(i)	Lower Primary Stage (Class I to V)	10%
(ii)	Upper Primary Stage (Class VI to VIII)	10%
(iii)	Secondary Stage (Class IX and X)	8%

The NPE (1986), has recommended for a minimum of 10 periods per week for physical education activities in lower primary and upper primary stages, and 7 periods per week at the secondary stage.

(iv) *Appointment of P.E.T.*: Every school should have a full time physical education teacher. The physical education teacher (PET) should be a trained person with B.A., B.P.Ed., qualification. He should also be deputed to attend inservice or refresher courses to update his knowledge and skill in physical education activities.

(v) *Organisation of Various Types of Programmes*: Physical education should aim at developing health, strength and fitness of students. Physical fitness has different components. Each of these components can be improved by participation in specific activities. Thus the school should organise different types of activities so that the aims of physical education can be achieved. Activities like running, swimming, basket-ball, foot-ball, volley-ball, hockey, cricket, jumping, relay race, throwing, balance exercises, dancing, hopscotch, gymnastics, drill, marching, callisthenics, yogasans, scouting and guiding can be organised depending upon the facilities available, age and interest of students and the ability and experience of PET. Every child should learn the rules of the game before he participates in a game. In every school intra-mural and extra-mural activities should be organised. In addition to regular physical education activities, inter-class competitions inter-group competitions, annual games and athletics meet, and inter-school meet should be organised in the school. Students should be encouraged and trained to participate in district level competitions. National School Games, and state level competitions.

(vi) *Evaluation of Performance*: The NPE (1986) has recommended to include sports and physical education in the evaluation of performance at different stages of education. Such evaluation will not only bring recognition to the talented students but it will motivate students for participation, performance and progress in such activities. The NPE recommends:

> "At the level of school education, assessment of participation and performance in sports and physical education activities may continue to be done in the form of grading. However the grade awarded to a child in sports and physical education should have the same weightage in the annual examination as it is attached to marks and grades in other subjects. Grades in physical education and sports corresponding to failure should be clearly identified."

6. ROLE OF THE HEADMASTER IN THE ORGANISATION AND MANAGEMENT OF PHYSICAL EDUCATION PROGRAMMES

The headmaster is the head of the institution. The success or failure of physical education programme of the school depends upon how the headmaster demonstrates his administrative and instructional leadership. He is the person who initiates, plans, implements and evaluates, supervises, guides and suggests ways and means of making the physical education programmes of the school attractive and successful. He has a major role to play in the organisation and management of physical education programme:

(i) He should study the philosophy, objectives, methods and materials of physical education thoroughly and accept it as an integral part of education.

(ii) He should see that the PET is trained in the art and science of physical education. If he finds that an untrained candidate was appointed as the PET as is the case in most private schools, he should take all steps to depute the teacher for undergoing training in physical education. Whether the PET is a trained person or an untrained person he should encourage the PET to attend inservice programmes, refresher courses, etc., to update his knowledge and skills in physical education.

(iii) He should make time allocations in the school time-table for physical education classes. At least 6 to 7 periods per week should be devoted for such classes. The headmaster should instruct the teacher in charge of time-table to allot physical education classes in the afternoon session of the school.

(iv) The headmaster should see that the school has a play ground of its own for conducting physical education classes. The playground should be kept neat and clean always. As far as possible the playground should have a boundary wall or fencing. Cows and other animals should not be allowed to gaze on the play ground as they may spoil the ground.

(v) If the school does not have a playground of its own but private or Government land adjacent to the school campus is available undisputed, then the headmaster should approach the owner of the land or move the government authority to spare the land for the school.

(vi) It is the duty of the headmaster to purchase the materials and equipment required for physical education purposes and hand over the same to the PET for use in physical education classes. The headmaster should not be satisfied with the limited resources provided by the management but convince business people, community leaders and government authorities for additional funds or assistance for better and qualitative organisation of physical education activities in the school.

(vii) The headmaster should supervise the physical education classes periodically and offer constructive suggestions for managing such classes in a better way. If the headmaster remains present in physical education classes occasionally this creates greater interest, alertness, and better performance on the part of the PET and the students.

(viii) He should monitor the progress in terms of the objectives of the curriculum from time to time.

(ix) He should create opportunity for organising various types of activities—indoor and outdoor, individual and group competitions according to the age and interest of students and the expertise of the PET. He should extend his support to the PET for organising intramural competitions, annual athletic meet and inter-school athletic meet. He should identify and encourage the talented students to participate in the district level competitions.

(x) He should give recognition to the winners and award prizes to them.

7. ROLE OF THE TEACHER IN THE ORGANISATION AND MANAGEMENT OF PHYSICAL EDUCATION CLASSES

Teachers have an important role to play in the organisation and management of physical education classes:

(i) The senior most teacher of the school should be a member of the School Committee for Physical Education.

(ii) All teachers should extend their co-operation for the smooth organisation and management of Physical Education Programme.

(iii) Teachers should discharge their duties and responsibilities assigned to them by the headmaster in connection with intramural competitions and annual athletic meet.

(iv) Each teacher must see that the students under his charge attend physical education classes regularly and with interest.

(v) Each teacher must try to encourage group competitions and individual competitions among his students while at the same time he must ensure a healthy interaction and relationship among students of various classes.

(vi) Teachers should participate and join in competitions meant for them in annual athletic meet of the school.

Some events in which they can participate are track and field events, yogasans and music chair.

(vii) In some schools the PET is not appointed. In some schools the post of PET remains vacant for years. In such cases one regular teacher of the school may conduct minimum programme of physical education in consultation and collaboration with the PET of a near-by school.

8. ROLE OF PHYSICAL EDUCATION TEACHER

Physical education teachers are teachers who are specialised in one particular educational field. They are educators first, and physical educators second, never the reverse. Thus a physical education teacher has to play the same role in the school and the society as any other teacher, but in addition to this he has to play a special role in his field of specialisation.

The physical education teacher should make a commitment to himself and to his students to serve individuals to attain the goals of education. He must have a desire to help students as they attempt through movement experiences, to become healthier, stronger, and more physically fit. He must realise that he is a stepping stone on the way to fulfilment of objectives of education.

The physical education teacher is a specialist teacher in physical education. So he is ultimately responsible for providing enjoyable opportunities for physical education activities. His specific role in this regard may be listed as follows:

(i) If he is untrained he should take initiative from his own side to undergo specialised training in physical education.

(ii) To play his role most effectively the PET must acquire and up-date his knowledge, skill and competencies by attending as many courses as possible.

(iii) He should plan his activities very carefully so that the objectives of physical education are achieved.

(iv) He should choose activities in keeping with the maturational level and interest of students.

(v) He should capitalise on interests already present and take notice of those that come about as a result of experience and exposure.

(vi) He should allow students to explore and discover activities for themselves.

(vii) He should organise indoor and outdoor activities, individual and group competitions, activities for boys and activities for girls, regular practice and intramural competitions.

(viii) While encouraging students for participation in such activities he should set purposeful progressive targets for each student.

(ix) He should see that any student who cannot safely or successfully participate in the regular physical education programme is provided with a programme in accordance with individual needs. This is particularly true in case of disabled children.

(x) He should organise two types of programmes for disabled children—Corrective Physical Education and Adaptive Physical Education, Corrective programmes are those programmes intended to correct or remedy a temporary handicapping condition. Helping in the rehabilitation of a fractural arm is one example of corrective physical education. Adaptive programmes are those programmes designed for individuals whose handicapping conditions are permanent. Creating meaningful movement experience for partially sighted, the blind and deaf children exemplifies adaptive programmes. Where a corrective programme is intended to remedy a temporary problem, an adaptive programme is intended to enable the individual to achieve his fullest movement potential within the limitations set by the permanent nature of the handicap.

(xi) The care and prevention of accidents/injuries in the field and the school is the primary task of physical education teachers. The teacher should endeavour to prevent athletic injuries. He should be skilled in caring for injuries. The physical education teacher is often the only qualified person available to render emergency assistance. He should, therefore, enroll in many intensive courses and emerge well qualified in the care and prevention of injuries.

(xii) The physical education teacher is the right person to identify the talented students and recommend for their further education and achievement. He should develop and maintain up-date records of individual talented students so that he can help them to receive advance coaching and participate in various competitions.

(xiii) The physical education teacher should manage intramural and inter-school programmes. Intramural programmes involve the creation and implementation of individual sports experiences, team sport experiences, leagues and tournaments. Interschool programmes involve inter-school athletic competitions wherein only highly skilled students participate. He is the person who extends his co-operation and provides his expertise in organising district competitions.

(xiv) In addition to organising and managing physical education classes he should help the headmaster to maintain order and discipline in the school. The physical education teacher must see that students learn behaviours such as punctuality, sincerity, regularity, co-operativeness, emotional tolerance, sensitivity to others' problems and difficulties, discipline, gentleness, etc., not only through physical education programmes but show these behaviours in all walks of their school life.

(xv) He should seek the co-operation and assistance of other teachers in organising various programmes of physical education. At the same time he should co-operate and assist other teachers in regular academic programmes of the school.

4

Yoga

1. THE CONCEPT OF YOGA

Every human being is a part of the all-pervading Divine Being which is the originator of the entire creation. We all are one and also of the same origin. Today everybody is at one another's throat to corner more and more wealth for himself. But there are people who have all the material comforts at their command but are unhappy and miserable. Are happiness and peace to be found in the enjoyment of luxuries and comforts of life? No, the real happiness can only be found in the pursuit of spiritual values. It depends upon the physical, mental and spiritual health of the people. Now the question arises how can we gain mental peace? How can we reduce the mental conflicts? The one and the only one answer to all those questions is to adopt yogic way of life which is inherited by us from our *rishis* and *munis* who struggle centuries after centuries and bestowed upon our culture the great science of Yoga.

The aim of man's life is to be free from worldly sorrows and to get submerged in the supreme soul and attain eternal bliss. A man suffers from sorrows and pains. To escape from these sorrows and to attain ultimate merger with the Eternal Being, man has to adopt yogic way of life.

The word 'Yoga' is derived from the root 'Yuj' which means union or merger. Thus yoga means "union of Atma and Paramattma (Divine Being)". It is the experience of oneness with God. According to the Bhagvat Gita the practice of yoga fixes the mind on God, thereby giving complete peace to the soul.

There are no better means than the yogic systems of purification to keep the body clean, healthy and beautiful. Our body has three basic properties: Vaat, Pitt, Kaph. If these three are present in the body to a balanced form, the body remains pure and disease-free. If this balance is disturbed, the body becomes susceptible to several kinds of diseases. Yogic exercises purify the body.

If the aim of yoga is the union of the individual soul with the Supreme Soul, it can be achieved through various ways. Consequently there are various types of yoga. Prominent among these types are:

- Gyan Yoga,
- Karma Yoga,
- Dhyan Yoga,
- Raj Yoga,
- Astang Yoga.

All lead to the same destination—Union with the Supreme Soul.

Astanga Yoga

Our *rishis* and *munis* have mentioned eight-fold process or Astang Yoga to attain the purification of body, mind and soul as well as to achieve union with the Supreme Being. Yoga involves eight processes or yoga has eight organs. These processes are:

(i) Yamas which means self-restraint. This manifests in *ahimsa, satya, asteya* (not to steal, not to be greedy), *brahmacharya* (control of senses, thought, words and deeds), *aparigraha* (non-covetousness).

(ii) Niyamas which mean religious observance. This manifests in *shaudha* (purity of mind), *santosha* (contentment), *tapa* (detachment and control of pleasure and pain feeling), *swadhyaya* (study of spiritual books), *Iswara pranldhana*, (complete surrender of self to God in words, deeds, and thought).

(iii) Asanas which mean sitting in a posture which is effortless and comfortable. There are two types of *asanas*:—meditative and physical.

(iv) Pranayama which means controlling the normal breathing cycle.

(v) Pratyahara which means withdrawal of the senses from their respective outside objects and projecting them inward.

(vi) Dharma which means fixing one's mind on an external object like heart, lotus, nose or one's favourite deity.

(vii) Dhyana which means meditation.

(viii) Samadhi which means a stage of super-consciousness and perfect calm.

2. YOGASANAS

Importance of Yogasanas

Yogasanas are of two types: meditative and physical. Those which involve mental activity are meditative, such as Padmasana, Sidhasana and Sukhasana, and those which are done primarily for keeping the body fit are physical asanas.

The aim is to keep both the mind and the body in perfect health through exercise of the body and the mind. The special feature of yogasanas is that what they do for the body, they do for the mind in a much more effective way. They are not only body-building exercises, more than that, they increase the mental powers. By achieving equanimity through asanas and pranayama we control our senses as well as our breathing, which is capable of lengthening life-span. More elastic our limbs, more healthy we are. In fact, elasticity is life. The age between 35 and 60 years is such that many of our limbs start becoming stiff and lose their elasticity. It is therefore most essential to take care of the body during this period. The old age disease, such as heart attack, blood pressure and diabetes generally attack a man during this period. Those who do not want to lose the chance of keeping their youth intact and their body health in perfect order should invariably practise yogasanas daily, so that the elasticity of limbs is maintained and the mental faculties do not disintegrate.

The impurities, which are formed due to the wear and tear

of the body and the accumulation of wastes after the food has been digested, find the following outlets: (i) through the nose in breath, (ii) through the anus in the form of excretes, (iii) through urine, and (iv) through the skin in the form of perspiration and dirt. Diseases are caused in the body when the impurities get accumulated in it. It is very obvious that if all these outlets are clean and open, and the wastes find their outlet properly through them, we can never fall ill. The regular practice of yogasanas keeps these outlets clean and open besides strengthening the organs which are responsible for excreting these impurities.

Some people, however, question why we should prefer yogasanas to other exercises such as gymnastic, wrestling and popular games. What about yogasanas? The following points will answer their queries:

1. Other exercises affect only the muscles outwardly, therefore, the body appears quite strong and healthy. But these exercises do not have as much impact on the internal organs of the body as the yogasanas. Yogasanas are very effective in throwing out all our body wastes and in activating our glands on the proper functioning of which depends our health and happiness. They give wonderful powers and increase longevity. Moreover in doing asanas the number of cells that break is small, while the number of new cells that are formed is proportionately very large.
2. Other exercises have very little impact on the mind and sense organs, while the asanas improve mental power and help in controlling the sense organs.
3. Yogasanas improve our resistance power against diseases and do not allow any external matter to accumulate in the body. In this way, they keep the body free from the diseases.
4. For sports and other exercises, we need considerable space and several persons. Asanas on the other hand can be performed in relatively little space and all by oneself. All that we need is a carpet or bed sheet. But we

must learn them first from a person who knows the technique well.

5. Yogasanas increase the elasticity of our body and make the body more active and subtle. The blood circulation takes place more smoothly and properly and the body becomes capable of more work. We look young in spite of our age. Other exercises, on the other hand, make the muscles stiff and hard. The body becomes stiff and the old age comes sooner.
6. As a drain is cleaned by sweeping and by putting water into it, the different asanas clean the blood-circulation drains of our body in the same way. Clean blood circulates freely in all parts of our body, and helps keep our body free from impurities. This is possible only by yogasanas and not by other exercises which increases our heartbeat abnormally. They do not have the capacity to clean the blood.
7. Our lungs are responsible for purifying our blood. By yogasanas and pranayama we increase the expansion and contraction of our lungs so that they become capable of purifying more and more blood. In other exercises, the lungs breathe quickly, but not deeply. The oxygen, therefore, does not reach their inner most parts. These parts, therefore, keep on accumulating wastes and impurities and after sometime show off as diseases.
8. We usually have an unnatural and wrong way of living in the modern times. We also eat unnatural food and thereby spoil our digestive system. The digestive organs cannot function properly due to this unnatural mode of living and eating. Yogasanas are the best means to keep these organs in proper functioning order. No other exercise can be a substitute for the asanas in this respect.
9. Our youth depends upon out spine which controls the entire nervous system and blood circulatory organs. The greater the elasticity in the vertebal column, the greater the vigour and longer life.

10. Other exercises cause tiredness to the body, while yogasanas make us fresh. In other exercises, the body has to spend a lot of energy, but in yogasanas it is not so, because these have to be done slowly by streatching the body limbs and then relaxing them. These exercises do not cause any violence to the body. They are, therefore, known as "non-violent exercises."
11. Other exercises have little impact on the character of a person. But yogasanas not only improve body health, they also have a sobering effect on the mind. They build-up mental and ethical powers. The mind becomes balanced and peaceful. This in turn brings about equanimity and sattuic ideas.
12. There are several glands in our body which keep us healthy and free from diseases if they function properly. Their secretion mix with blood and the man becomes healthy and strong. For example, if thyroid and parathyroid glands which are located in the neck do not secrete their juices in the required quantity, the children's development is halted and even young men start losing their hair prematurely. The practice of yogasana is very effective in activating these glands, so that they secrete their juices in the required quantity.
13. In fact, yogasanas, pranayama and six yogic practices of purification are a panacea for all ills. They have a unique power to throw waste products out of the body. They can, therefore, be depended upon for physical and mental well-being.
14. Besides having physical, mental and moral effects, yoga system leads a man to spiritualism. No other system has such wide-ranging impact on human body, mind, brain and intellect.

Selected Yogasanas

1. Padmasana

Place your left foot on joint of your right thigh, and the right foot on the joint of left thigh in such a way that both your heels touch each other below your navel in the middle of your abdomen. In this way, soles of your feet will stay on your thighs. Now, straighten your backbone and neck so that there is no bend at your waist. Place your hands on your knees.

2. Sidhasana

Place the heel of your left foot under the testes on the prostrate gland in such a way that the sole of your foot should touch your right thigh. Place the heel of your right foot aganist the pubic bone or just above the genitals. Now straighten your neck and backbone and raise your brows. Fix your attention on your eyebrows or on your breath. Place your hands as in Padmasana.

3. Ardha Chandrasanas

Stand erect with joined heels. Take the hand above your head and join them in the posture of *namaskar*. Inhale and bend towards left from the waist. Exhale and bring the body back in the straight position. Repeat this by bending the body towards right.

In stretching the muscles on both side this asana makes the body flexible. It improves the functioning of the heart and the lungs. The liver, the stomach and the intestines are also strengthened by its practice. It improves digestion and increases appetite. It gives relief to those suffering from sciatica.

4. Vajrasana

Bend your legs and sit on your knees by placing your heels under your hips. The heels should be open but the toes should be joined and the feet would be all on the ground. Now make your spine straight, place your hands on your kness while keeping the arms straight. You can sit in this posture at any time of the day even after eating your food or after traveling a long distance. This will give rest to your tired legs. You can practise it while reading also. This asana is as useful as it is easy.

This assana has good effect on our digestive system. The impurities accumulated in our spine and knees are displaced.

5. Bhujangasana

Lie down with your face downward, touching the ground with your forehead. Let your palms touch the ground just below your shoulders and as wide apart as your chest. Now raise your elbow a little. Start inhaling and raising the front part up to your navel. Give maximum curve to your chest and abdomen and look up in the sky. Do not separate your heels. Stay in this posture for sometime and then come back to the original position, exhaling. Keeping your left cheek on the ground, leave the body in relaxed state.

It is specially an useful asana for the kidneys. The neck, shoulders and spine get strength. The glands of the neck and tonsils get influenced favourably. The body gets youthful elasticity. It causes an abundant flow of blood towards the backbone. It is very useful asana for strengthening the heart.

6. Shashankasana

Sit in Vajrasana. Inhale and raise both the hands up above the head. The palms should point forward. Exhale and place the hands on the ground while bending slowly from the waist. The forehead should also touch the ground a little away from the kness. Stay in this posture for atleast one minute and then relax completely.

This is an asana of relaxation. It calms the disturbed mind and gives strength and energy to the brain. Negative feeling of anger, hatred, etc., are gradually relieved by its constant practice.

Rest Posture

While doing sitting asanas, practise 'rest posture' after every asana. This will normalize breath and bring the stretched limbs, muscles and nerves to their original positions. In this posture one must leave the body in a completely relaxed state so that pure blood should circulate in the body and force the waste material out. This is the secret of health.

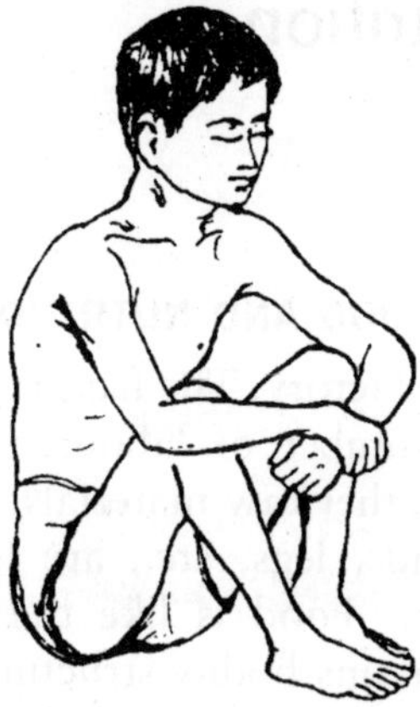

5

Food and Nutrition

1. IMPORTANCE OF FOOD AND NUTRITION

Our body is like a factory. The factory needs different types of machines and a number of labourers. The factory needs water, coal, iron and other raw materials. Our eyes, ears, nose, mouth, stomach, hands, legs, etc., are like the machines or labourers in a factory. Food is like the raw material. Food provides energy, maintains bodily structures and function, and promotes growth. Good food is needed for a person to grow, work hard and stay healthy. Many common sicknesses come from not eating enough of the food the body needs. Poor nutrition is the most common cause of the following problems:

In Children

(i) Failure of a child to grow or gain weight normally.

(ii) Slowness in walking, talking or thinking.

(iii) Swollen bellies, thin arms and legs.

(iv) Sadness, lack of energy.

(v) Swelling of feet, face and hands, often with sores or marks on the skin.

(vi) Loss of hair, or loss of its colour or shine.

(vii) Dryness of eyes, blindness.

In Any One

(i) Weakness and tiredness.

(ii) Loss of appetite.

(iii) Anemia (this happens when blood is lost or destroyed faster than the body can replace it).

(iv) Sores in the corners of the mouth.

(v) Painful or sore tongue.

(vi) 'Burning' or numbness of the feet.

Although the following problems may have other causes, they are often caused or made worse by not eating well:

- Diarrhoea,
- Ringing or buzzling in the ears,
- Headache,
- Bleeding or redness of the gums,
- Nose bleeding,
- Stomach discomfort,
- Dryness and craking of the skin,
- Fits or convulsions in small children,
- Heavy pulsing of the heart,
- Anxiety and various nerve and mental problems,
- Liver disease,
- Frequent infections.

Not eating well may be the direct cause of the health problems just listed. But, in addition, poor nutrition weakens the body's ability to restrict all kinds of diseases, especially infections. Eating right helps the body resist sickness. Not only does good food help prevent disease, it also helps the sick body fight disease and become well again. So during and after any sickness, it is very important to eat nutritious food. Eating well and keeping clean are the best guarantees of good health.

Food provides energy to keep the body warm, the muscles active for work and play, and the various organs alert to carry out the daily activities.

Food stuffs may be broadly classified under three heads, *viz.*, energy-yielding, body-building, and protective food stuffs according to the predominant role they play in sustaining life.

Energy-yielding food stuffs form the great bulk of the ordinary diet. They are known as 'fuel-foods'. A few examples of energy-yielding food stuffs are cereals, starchy vegetables, pulses, nuts, sugars and oil.

Food also supplies building material needed for growth. During infancy, childhood and adolescence new tissues are being continuously built and the 'wear and tear' tissues are to be repaired every day. Hence there is a tremendous demand for building materials.

Body building food stuffs contain a satisfactory amount of the nutrients needed to build the body and replace the worn out tissues. Milk and its products, meat, fish and eggs, grams, dals, dried beans, peas and nuts and cereals are the best representative of this group.

Food has also protective function. Some food stuffs help in protecting the body from disease and abnormal development or stunted growth. If the diet is deficient or lacking in one or more of these vital substances it leads to disturbance of the normal functioning of the different parts of the body, resulting in ill-health, stunted growth and imperfect development.

Food and nutrition do not mean the same thing. Something may be called food but it may not have any nutritional value. For example, coffee may be regarded as food but it has no nutritional value. Different types of food have different nutritional values. Food contains the following nutrients:

- Protein,
- Fat,
- Carbohydrate,
- Mineral substances, and
- Vitamins.

All these nutrients are not present in the same source or food. Different nutrients are found from different sources. Thus food may be classified under different groups depending upon the nutrients. It is desirable that we should eat enough from different food groups instead of enough of a particular food. Variety of items in a meal is more beneficial than plenty of a single food item in a meal.

2. THE NUTRIENTS OF FOOD

Food contains the following nutrients: protein, fat, carbohydrate, mineral substances and vitamins.

Protein

Protein is an essential constituent of all animal and vegetable cells. Protein is used in the body for growth and for repair of waste, and is, therefore of particular importance to the growing child. It is also a source of energy. When taken into the body, protein is broken down by digestion into amino-acids. These represent so many different components out of which the protein molecule is built; one protein molecule may contain as many as twenty of them. Probably atleast ten amino-acids are essential for the growth of the child; they must be supplied in the food, as they cannot be made by the body. All these essential amino-acids are present in anyone molecule of animal protein; in some vegetable proteins, however, one or more will be absent, though a suitable mixture of vegetable proteins may supply them all. If the amino-acids are to be fully used in building up the fresh proteins needed in the body, a complete assertment of them should be available in the diet. When milk, meat and choose are scanty, they should be spread over several meals and eaten with bread, potatoes and cereal in order that the fullest possible use may be made of the amino-acids in the diet.

Fat

Fat is found in all animal fats, such as meat fat, butter fat, and oils. It is an important source of energy and heat. In animals, fat may be formed from carbohydrate.

Carbohydrate

Carbohydrate is the nutrient which supplies energy; it can be converted into fat. It occurs in foodstuffs in two forms, sugar and starch:

(i) *Sugar*: Glucose is the simplest form of sugar. Other forms of sugar such as fructose, lactose, sucrose and maltose are broken down to glucose by digestion in the alimentary tract. The molecules of glucose are then absorbed into the blood stream through the mucous membrane lining the small intestine.

(ii) *Starch*: Starch is a compound molecule containing many molecules of glucose. It is also broken down by digestion to glucose, and is then absorbed by the alimentary tract.

Starches and sugars are found chiefly in sugar, flour, bread, fruits and vegetables.

Minerals

Nineteen major inorganic substances (mineral) are contained in the body, all of which must be derived from food. Minerals are important in the formation of bones and teeth (especially calcium, phosphorus and magnesium), as constituents of body cells, and as soluble salts in tissue fluids. In addition iodine is concerned in thyroid metabolism, copper and iron in red blood cell formation, and cobalt in combating anemia (vitamin B_{12}). Most of these minerals are needed only in very small amounts; they are widely distributed in nature.

Vitamins

Vitamins are organic substances necessary for life and health; they are found in very small amounts in natural foods. Some of the vitamins (e.g. A.D.E. and K) are found mainly in fatty foods, and are called fat-soluble; others (e.g. B complex and C) are water-soluble, Vitamins were discovered early in the twentieth century; their chemical structures were not known for some years. They were named after the letters of the alphabet, or simply referred to as "factors" preventing certain diseases, e.g. vitamin D was known as the anti-rachitic vitamin. After recent advances in biochemistry we can now assign chemical formulae to several of the vitamins, and many of them can be synthesised in the laboratory: vitamin B, for example, was first produced synthetically in 1948.

Vitamin A occurs in certain fats and in the fatty parts of some foods. Carotene, a precursor of vitamin A, is found in certain vegetable food-stuffs. Carotene can be changed into vitamin A in the human body, but less efficiently than in the bodies of some animals; that is why animal sources of vitamin A are more effective than vegetable sources. Vitamin A is necessary in the body for growth, it is concerned in the perception of light, and it protects skin and mucous surfaces of the body from infection. If it is not well represented in the diet, bodily health will suffer. An excess of vitamin A, however, will not improve health; enough is as good as a feast.

The following are the sources of vitamin A: they are listed (like the other vitamin sources given in this section) in order of potency, beginning with the most potent source and ending with the least:

(i) *Animal*: Haliburt liver oil, cod-liver oil, ox-liver, butter, margarine, cheese, eggs, sardine, herring.

(ii) *Vegetable*: Carrot, spinach, watercress, apricot, tomatoes, prunes.

Vitamin D is concerned with the laying down of calcium and phosphorus in bone; it is therefore of particular importance during periods of rapid growth. Too little of this vitamin may cause rickets; too much may cause metabolic disturbances in infants. It may be obtained from food, or it may be formed in the skin by the action of sunlight. It is contained in cod-liver oil, sardines, herring, tinned salmon, margarine, eggs and butter. Like vitamin A, it is fat-soluble and heat resistant.

Vitamin E is necessary for normal reproduction in rats, but we do not know whether it plays any part in the fertility of human beings. It is found in milk, in wheat germ, and (in small amounts) in green vegetables.

Vitamin K is essential for the normal clotting of blood. It is found in green plants such as peas and cabbage.

Vitamin B group of Nutrients: All members of the group are water-soluble; they are widely distributed in food stuffs, and are often found together. At one time only two components were recognised, Vitamin B_2 and Vitamin B_{12}. Today (1956) about twelve vitamins have been described though it is not certain that all of them are necessary to the human economy.

Aneurin or thiamin (*Vitamin* B_2) is concerned in the mechanism of releasing energy from carbohydrate. If there is not enough of this vitamin in the diet, growth is checked, a particular form of neurities may develop, and there may be depression and irritability. If the deficiency in severe and prolonged, as it was in Japanese prisoner-of-war camps during the last war, beri-beri develops.

Riboflavin is also concerned in the process of obtaining energy from carbohydrate for use by the body. If it is of short supply, growth is slowed down and cracks and sores may appear at the corners of the mouth, with the tongue becoming red and raw, and the cornea hazy.

Nicotinic acid (*Vitamin B_2*) is also concerned in releasing energy from carbohydrate. When there is not enough of this vitamin in the diet, growth is checked, the skin is liable to become rough and red, and the tongue may be red and sore. If deficiency is severe and prolonged, diarrhoea and dementia may occur (pellagra).

Some other members of the B group are:

Pyridoxine, needed for growth, health of skin and protein metabolism.

Pantothenic acid, necessary for growth and health of the skin.

Biotin, concerned with health of the skin.

Folic acid, concerned with growth: it is used in treatment of macrocytic anaemia.

B_{12} used in treatment of pernicious anemia, is found in animal foods only, particularly milk, eggs and cheese. The other members of the vitamin B group are found together in the following food stuffs.

Bread, meat (pork contains about ten times more B than beef or mutton), liver, yeast, oatmeal, green peas, peanuts, potatoes, meat extract, cheese, eggs, malt and milk.

Milk is an important source of riboflavin, and bread less good one.

Vitamin C (*Ascorbic acid*) is concerned with the maintenance of the integrity of the connective tissue structures. If it is in short supply, growth will be checked, the gums and mouth will be liable to infection, healing will be slowed; prolonged deprivation is likely to lead to scurvy. This vitamin is found mainly in fruit and vegetables, is easily destroyed by cooking, and tends to deteriorate if food is stored. Ascorbic acid exists in high concentration in rapidly growing vegetables; new potatoes contain more of it than old potatoes. It is well represented in blackcurrants, sprouts, cauliflower, cabbage, watercress, orange, lemon, grapefruit and potato. Since fruits and vegetables tend to be expensive in the winter, the diet may easily be low in ascorbic acid. Great care must be taken to see that a good supply of this vicamin is available in diet.

It will be noticed that all the vitamins are essential to growth. Vitamins are needed only in small amounts; if an adequate amount of any particular vitamin is available in the diet, no benefit will be reaped by taking more. Various vitamin preparations are on the market. They have their uses, and are particularly valuable when food supplies are limited (as in time of war). In general, however, it is better to take the natural products whenever they are available.

3. MALNUTRITION

What is malnutrition?

To be healthy and strong a person needs to eat enough foods from each of the food groups. Many people eat large amounts of starchy energy foods like rice, chapatti, potato, but not enough of body building and protective foods like beans, peas, pulses, dark greeny leafy vegetables and fruits. These people can be malnourished. Malnutrition refers to health problems caused by not eating enough of the foods which the body needs. It is a pathological state resulting from a relative or absolute deficiency or excess of one or more essential nutrients. Malnutrion is often most severe in children who need lots of nutritious food to grow well and stay healthy.

Two terms—undernutrition and overnutrition—are often used to explain malnutrition. Undernutrition refers to deficiency of nutritious food the body needs. Overnutrition refers to an excess of a particular nutrient in the food. The two most common forms of severe malnutrition are the following: (i) Kwashiorkor or wet malnutrition, and (ii) Marasmus or dry malnutrition.

Kwashiorkor or wet malnutrition results from not eating enough protein. Marasmus or dry malnutrition results from not eating enough food. The following symptoms indicate whether the child has wet malnutrition or dry malnutrition.

Symptoms of wet malnutrition

- Swollen 'moon' face.
- Miserable health.
- Loss of growth.
- Sores and peeling skin.
- Swollen hands and feet.
- Loss of colour in hair and skin.
- Thin upper arms.
- The child is skin, bones, and water.

Symptoms of dry malnutrition:

- Face of an old man.
- Always hungry.
- Pot belly.
- Very underweight.
- Very thin.
- The child is just *skin* and *bones*.

Often a child may show the signs of wet malnutrition and dry malnutrition at the same time. His legs may be swollen as in wet malnutrition, but his arms may be thin as in dry malnutrition. The child needs more food.

Harmful Effects of Malnutrition

Malnutrition has a number of harmful effects upon children and expectant mothers. These effects are of two types: Specific effects which are related to deficiency of a particular nutrient, and general effects. The specific effects of malnutrition are given in Table 1. There are a number of food deficiency diseases of which the following deserve mention:

Table 1: Specific Effects of Malnutrition

Nutrient	Effect of deficiency
Carbohydrate	Loss of weight, acidosis
Certain factty acids	Skin disorders (eczema)
Protein	Kwashiorkor, anaemia
Vitamin A	Xerophthalmia, blindness
Thiamine (B_1)	Beriberi
Nicotinic acid	Pellagra
Riboflavin (B_2)	Vascularization of cornea, Circum corneal infection, Chelosis, angular stomatitis
Vitamin C	Scurvy
Vitamin D	Rickets
Vitamin E	Sterility, eye abnormalities
Vitamin K	Failure of blood clotting
Calcium	Rickets
Iron	Anaemia
Iodine	Goitre

General Effects of Malnutrition

1. Malnutrition is the biggest single contributor to child mortality in the developing world.
2. Malnutrition adversely affects mental development, physical development, productivity, the span of working years.... Malnutrition during the fetal period and in infancy is associated with intellectual impairment.
3. Malnutrition interferes with a child's motivation, ability to concentrate, and ability to learn, whatever its ultimate effect on the condition of the brain itself. Learning time is lost during the most critical periods of learning. A malnourished child is listless, lacking in curiosity, and unresponsive to material and other stimulation.
4. The nutritional anaemias of mothers extend precarious health to the newborn: stillbirths and premature births are much more common among anaemic mothers, and premature children are much more likely to die.

5. The widest and most lasting impact, however, probably would come from providing adequate nutrition to mothers in the last trimester of pregnancy—the critical period for fetal growth—and the children six months through two or three years of age (most of the needs before six months can be met through breast feeding). The greatest physiological need and the greatest growth occur in the early ears: 80 per cent of eventual brain weight, for example, is reached by age 2.

Care and Treatment of Deficiencies and Diseases due to Malnutrition

As is true with other types of health problems, prevention is better than cure in dealing with malnutrition. The care and treatment of malnutrition require the following steps:

(i) Medical examination of children at intervals.

(ii) School feeding programme.

(iii) Parent education programme.

(iv) Co-operation between the school and the community.

(v) Help and assistance by voluntary agencies and Government departments.

(vi) Development of proper food habits among children.

In the treatment of malnutrition the first step is to ascertain the cause by carrying out a thorough medical examination of the child, and by ascertaining from the parents the child's modes of living. Any disease or deficiency discovered by medical personnel will require treatment. Errors of diet should be corrected. The school doctor may visit the child's home and advise the mother how to carryout any instruction given by the medical personnel with regard to diet, sleeping, accommodation, ventilation, etc. The school can contribute to this by organising special courses on diets, cooking and preparing nutritious food at low cost.

Due to poverty of parents most children in rural and tribal areas are found undernourished. As an immediate remedy for undernourishment school feeding is to be provided. It is left to the teacher to pick-out those children who appear to be undernourished and to draw the attention of the school medical personnel.

It has been observed that due to ill-balanced diet people of all ages generally suffer from ill-health. Among school children the condition of malnutrition due to unsatisfactory diet at home can be more or less corrected by means of providing suitable mid-day meal.

Teachers must select the children who are malnourished and prescribe diet for them. The doctor may supplement or correct lists prepared by teachers. He should often examine the children in the school or note their conditions during visits to the feeding centre.

The best measure in the care and treatment of malnutrition is parent education programme. Parents should be educated about the importance of different food groups, quantity of food, balanced diet, proper food habits and all hygienic conditions. It is not right to think that nutritious food is very expensive and as ordinary parents cannot provide better food to their children. In fact, better foods can be provided at low cost to anyone for purpose of ensuring health and strength.

Prevention and cure of malnutrition is not the sole responsibility of the school. Unless the community co-operates with the school, unless government and voluntary agencies extend their help, assistance, and expertise the school cannot treat nor prevent malnutrition.

Overnutrition

Malnutrition is noticed mainly in two forms—under nutrition and overnutrition. As the two terms imply, under nutrition means deficiency of some nutrients and overnutrition is excess of some nutrients. Undernutrition is the condition which results when insufficient food is eaten over an extended period of time. In extreme cases it is called starvation.

Just as undernutrition refers to deficiency of some nutrients in the food one eats so also overnutrition results from excess of nutrients in the food. Undernutrition is a major problem of under developed countries. Overnutritioin is a major problem of developed countries. The poor people suffer from under nutrition. But overnutrition is generally found among the rich people.

Overnutrition is the pathological state resulting from the consumption of excessive quantity of food over an extended period of time. Malnutrition in the form of overnutrition makes a person obese. Obesity is one of the major health hazards in developed countries and also in case of people of higher economic strata of our country. Overeating and calorie excess are the contributing factors for obesity. Obesity leads to diseases like diabetes, high blood pressure, joint problems, heart diseases, menstural irregularities and infertility.

4. BALANCED DIET

In order to prevent the harmful effects of malnutrition and to sustain a vigorous and healthy life it is necessary to know the daily requirements of nutrients and the proper diet for children. In fact the daily requirements of nutrients or the 'proper diet' will vary with factors such as age, sex and the type of work.

The diet for children should be so planned that it would provide the essential nutrients in the needed amount and proportions. A diet which contains different types of foods in such quantities and proportions that the need for calories, proteins, fat, minerals, vitamins and other nutrients is adequately met is called a balanced diet. In other words, diet which contains energy-yielding food, body-building food and protective food in right quantity and proportion to meet the needs of the body is called a balanced diet. A balanced diet, therefore, contains enough food of different varieties which the body needs. The quantity and proportions of items in a balance diet vary depending upon the age and occupation of the individual.

Balanced diet as recommended by the Indian Council of Medical Research (1968), for boys and girls in different age groups is given in the following Tables.

TABLE 2: Balanced Diet for Pre-school Children (In Grams)

Food	(1 to 3 years)		(3 to 6 years)	
	Vegetarian	Non-Veg.	Vegetarian	Non-Veg.
Cereals	150	150	200	200
Pulses	50	40	60	50
Green leafy Vegetables	50	50	75	74
Other Vegetables	30	30	50	50
Fruits	50	50	50	50
Milk	300	200	250	200
Fats/Oil	20	20	25	25
Meat/Fish/Eggs	—	30	—	30
Sugar and Juggery (Gura)	30	30	40	40
Roots and Tubers	—	—	—	—
Ground Nuts	—	—	—	—

TABLE 3: Balanced Diet Primary School Children (In Grams)

Food	(6 to 9 years)		(9 to 12 years)	
	Vegetarian	Non-Veg.	Vegetarian	Non-Veg.
Cereals	250	250	320	320
Pulses	70	60	70	60
Green Leafy Vegetables	75	75	100	100
Other Vegetables	50	50	50	75
Fruits	50	50	50	50
Milk	250	200	250	200
Fats/Oil	30	30	35	35
Meat/Fish/Eggs	—	30	—	30
Sugar and Juggery (Gura)	40	50	50	50
Roots and Tubers	—	—	—	—
Ground Nuts	—	—	—	—

TABLE 4: Balanced Diet for High School Children (In Grams)

Food	(12 to 15 years)				(15 to 18 years)			
	Vegetarian		Non-Veg.		Vegetarian		Non-Veg.	
	Boys	Girls	Boys	Girls	Boys	Girls	Boys	Girls
Cereals	430	350	430	350	450	350	450	350
Pulses	70	70	50	50	70	70	50	50
Green Leafy Vegetables	100	150	100	150	100	150	100	150
Other Vegetables	75	75	75	75	75	75	75	75
Fruits	30	30	30	30	30	30	30	30
Milk	250	250	150	150	250	250	150	150
Fats/Oil	35	35	40	40	45	35	50	40
Meat/Fish/Eggs	—	—	30	30	—	—	30	30
Sugar and Juggery (Gura)	30	30	30	30	40	30	40	30
Roots and Tubers	75	75	75	75	100	75	100	75
Ground Nuts	50	—	50	—	50	—	50	—

5. PROPER FOOD HABITS

One of the objectives of health education is to develop proper health habits and practices in young children. Among all health habits, proper food habits deserve the attention of parents and teachers.

Habits are learned tendencies of the individual. They are not innate tendencies. No child in born with any habit. Habits of cleanlinss, habits of taking food, etc., are learned by the child in the home and the school. In other words, the child learns food habits in the environment in which he is brought up—from parents, siblings and other children in the home and the school. Proper or improper food habits are the result of training, guidance and reinforcement provided to the child during the formative years of his life. Proper food habits mean many things:

- how to eat?
- what to eat?

- when to eat?
- where to eat?
- why to eat? etc.

How to eat food?

It is very important to teach children, especially young babies, to wash hands and mouth before and after a meal. The baby should learn to eat food not with both hands or the left hand but with the right hand. Sometimes appetite and digestion may fail because of worry and anxiety. A meal should be a serene and sociable affair. Meal should be served in a pleasant orderly way in surroundings which are civilized and amicable. There should not be any sense of strain, rush or emotional distress during dinner so that the meal can be enjoyed depending upon the flavour, cooking, service, and the company. As far as possible everyone should follow the, 'table manners' which add to the beauty and gentleness to the scene.

It sometimes happens that insistence on a standard of behaviour or the 'table manners' beyond their age is a cause of under-feeding and feeding difficulties in young children. To attempt to 'civilise' at a primitive stage will only cause strain for all concerned. Feeding is a natural bodily function and in the early years should be treated as such. The less children have to think about it, the better.

What to eat?

Children should have a variety of items in their meal. The body needs different nutrients for its growth, energy and protection. Thus instead of serving the same item of food every day, different items, varieties of items should be served on different days. In fact a balanced diet is a necessity for young children for their healthy growth, energy and protection from diseases.

Some food items are very expensive. That is why most parents hesitate to provide expensive food items like meat, fish or egg to their children. But most parents are ignorant about "better foods at cheaper costs". For example, herring supplies nearly as much body building food as the same weight of salmon and herring is cheaper than salmon. The cheaper kinds of cheese contains rather more body-building material than the more expensive sorts and are easier to digest. There are no healthier or cheaper green vegetables than kale, cabbage or spring greens. An orange is a better food than a peach. Thus parents must be educated about preparing better foods at cheaper costs.

A child should not be forced to eat food he dislikes. Likes and dislikes should not be discussed in a child's hearing but should be noticed and taken into account when planning the dietary.

When to eat?

As a general rule, it is convenient for family meals to be served at stated times and regular intervals. But occasionally babies and small children are allowed to go hungry in order to conform to an arbitrary time-table of meals. Such harshness fails to take into consideration their emotional and physical needs. When small children are hungry they should be fed, and there is no other rule that matters. As they grow older they should be more able to conform to adult conventions regarding fixed hours for meals. Thus four principles are to be followed regarding the time of meals:

(i) Food should be served, usually, at regular time and intervals;

(ii) Babies and small children should be allowed to eat whenever they are hungry;

(iii) No one should remain in an empty stomach for a long time;

(iv) One should not be forced to eat when he is not hungry.

Where to eat?

One crucial point about proper food habits is the place of eating. Food should be eaten at a place which is neat and clean, and free from dust, insects and germs. Whether it is a dinning room, floor, or a hotel, the place must be kept neat and clean. One should avoid to eat food at places which are dirty and full of dust, insects or germs. Children should be discouraged to eat food in dirty hotels, streets, melas or market places as these places are in unhygienic conditions. If food is taken in a dinning room, it should be kept pleasant, sociable and little decorative.

Why to eat food?

Children should be educated about the importance of food, values of different nutrients, and the effects of their deficiency or excess. Children should be encouraged to develop proper attitude towards different types of food and nutrients. Such education about the importance of different nutrients—different items in the food should be provided by parents incidentally and formally by teachers in the school.

References

FAO. *Lives in peril - protein and the child*. Rome 1970, p. 25.

Bert, Alan, *The nutrition factor, its role in national development,* Washington, D.C. 1973, p. 9.

Ibid., p. 11.

Ibid., p. 16.

Ibid., p. 24.

6

First Aid and Safety

FIRST AID

1. WHAT IS FIRST AID?

First-aid is defined as the immediate and temporary care given to the victim of an accident or sudden illness in order to avert complications, lessen suffering and sustain the person until the services of a physician is obtained. The first-aider should not regard himself as a substitute for a physician. He should understand that his primary duty is to provide immediate and temporary care to the victim until the physician is available. By providing immediate and temporary care the first-aider can achieve three primary objectives:

(i) to avert complications,

(ii) to lessen suffering, and

(iii) to save life.

Essentials of first-aid

The person rendering first-aid should follow certain general instructions which are the essentials of all first-aid activities:

(i) Keep the first aid equipments ready for use.

(ii) Avoid excitement or panic.

(iii) Correct situations that might aggrevate the original injury.

(iv) Protect the victim from unnecessary exposure to the elements or to new hazards.

(v) Do not move the prostrate victim until the approximate nature of the injury has been determined.

(vi) Keep the victim lying in a comfortable position; his head levels with his body.

(vii) Look for cases like serious bleeding, stoppage of breathing, poisoning, wounds, fractures, dislocations, etc., and treat them immediately.

(viii) Try to elicit response from the victim.

(ix) Never have a patient stand or walk until the first-aider has determined that there is no injury to the spine, pelvis or legs.

(x) Keep the injured person warm. He should have blankets under him.

(xi) Never give water or other liquids to an unconscious person.

(xii) Do not allow the patient see his own injury.

(xiii) Send someone to call a physician or ambulance.

(xiv) Make use of a stretcher for transportation of the patient.

(xv) Do not act in a hurry. Act carefully. Improper action might increase the damage.

2. COMMON INJURIES/ACCIDENTS AND MEASURES OF FIRST AID.

FRACTURE

Fracture is a break in a bone. It is generally the result of accidents such as a fall or a sudden blow. X-ray examination is the only positive way for determining the nature and extent of any injury. There are two kinds of fractures:

(i) Closed or simple fracture in which the bone is broken without any injury to the surrounding tissues, and

(ii) Open or compound fracture in which the bone is broken resulting in injury to the tissues including the skin so that germs may enter into the injured part. Compound fracture is much more serious than the simple fracture.

The most common symptoms of fracture are:

(i) Tenderness and swelling over the injured bone.

(ii) Pain on moving the injured part.

(iii) Loss of power of the injured part to work.

Treatment

(i) Where a bone is broken—the most important thing to do is to keep the bone in a fixed position. This prevents more damage and lets it mend.

(ii) Before trying to move or carry a person with a broken bone, keep the bones from moving with splints, strips of bark, or a sleeve of cardboard. Later a plaster cast can be put on the limb at a health center, or perhaps you can make a 'cast' according to local traditions.

(iii) If the bones seem more or less in the right position, it is better not to move them. This could do more harm than good. If the bones are far out position and the break is recent, you can try to set or strengthen them before putting on a cast. The sooner the bones are set, the easier it will be. It is possible to do a lot of damage while trying to set a bone. Ideally, it should be done with the help of someone with experience.

(iv) If there is no one with experience in setting bones call for the doctor immediately. The injured person should be moved to the hospital in a stretcher very carefully.

(v) Never rub or message a broken limb or a limb that may possibly be broken.

(vi) The worse the break or the older the person, the longer healing takes. Children's bones mend rapidly. Those of old people sametimes never join. A broken arm should be kept in a cast for about a month, and no force put on it for another month. A broken leg should remain in a cast for about two months.

DISLOCATIONS

Dislocations refer to bones that have come out of place at joint. It is caused mainly by a jerk, sudden fall or out-stretching of hand or leg. Dislocation may occur in case of shoulder, elbow, knee, lower jaw and other joint places. The most common symptoms of dislocations are as follows:

(i) Pain in the joint.

(ii) Swelling over the affected part.

(iii) Loss of power of the limb to work.

Treatment

(i) Try to put the bone back into the place. The sooner the better.

(ii) Keep it bandaged firmly in place so that it does not slip out again (about a month).

(iii) Avoid forceful use of the limb long enough for the joint to heal completely (2 or 3 months).

(iv) Call for a doctor for treatment or move the patient to the nearest health centre. The longer you wait, the harder it will be to correct.

POISONING

Poisoning is more frequently noticed in rural areas, although it is also noticed in urban areas. Poisoning may occur intentionally or due to ignorance of the poisonous effects of some substance which are used in day-to-day life. Some common poisons to watch out for are as follows:

- rat poison;
- DDT, lindane, sheep dip, and other insecticides;
- medicine (any kind when much is swallowed);
- tincture of iodine;
- bleach and detergents;
- cigarettes;
- poisonous leaves, seeds or berries;
- paints;
- unused matches—the tips are poisonous, kerosene, gasoline, petrol;
- lye.

There are some poisonous matters which burn body tissues. These are called corrosive poison. Poisonous matters which do not burn body tissues are called non-corrosive poison. These poisonous matters may be taken through the following ways;

(i) through the mouth while eating;

(ii) through the nose by inhailing the gas;

(iii) through the skin by contact.

After taking poison the person may remain conscious or unconscious. If you suspect poisoning do the following immediately.

Treatment for a Conscious Person

(i) Make the person vomit. Put your finger in his throat, or tickle the back of his throat with a spoon, or make him drink warm water with a lot of salt in it.

(ii) If the person does not vomit, lay the person on a cot. Put in a well greased stomach tube through the mouth and pour in 1 to 2 litres of water through the funnel. Lower the end of the stomach tube below the level of the bed. The liquid in the stomach will come out. Continue doing this till the liquid coming out is clean.

(iii) Have him drink all he can of milk, beaten eggs, or flour mixed with water. If you have it, give him a tablespoon of powdered charcot, keep giving him more milk, eggs, or flour and water, and keep him vomiting until the vomit is clear.

Treatment of an Unconscious Persons

(i) Do not make him vomit. If he has stopped breathing, then give mouth-to-mouth breathing.

(ii) Seek medical help at once.

(iii) Cover the person if he feels cold, but avoid too much heat.

Do not make a person vomit if he has swallowed kerosene, gasoline, petrol, or strong acids or corrosive substances like lye.

Pesticide Poisoning

Pesticides are substances used to kill the various pests like insects, rats, weeds etc., that destroy the cultivated crops, or spread diseases (flies, mosquitoes) Poisoning occurs when people carelessly handle the pesticides and do not take the necessary precautions, or when the person does not cover his nose and mouth when spraying pesticide, or if the person does not cover all his food and drinking water when his house is being sprayed.

Signs of Pesticide Poisoning

- Headache;
- Vomiting;
- Abdominal pain;
- Convulsions;
- Signs of shock;
- Difficulty in breathing;
- Loss of consciousness.

If first-aid is not given immediately, the person will die.

Treatment

(i) Remove the person from risk of further exposure,

(ii) If he has convulsions give him a sedative and protect him from harm and from biting his tongue,

(iii) Rush him to the health centre fast.

Precaution to prevent poisoning

(i) Never keep kerosene, gasoline, or other poisions in cola or soft drink bottles, because children may try to drink them.

(ii) Keep all poisons out of reach of children.

(iii) Wear rubber gloves, or wrap your hands in a polythene paper while handling the pesticides.

(iv) If you are spraying the pesticides, cover your nose and mouth with a cloth.

(v) Wash your hands well with soap and water after handling any pesticides.

(vi) Cover all your food and drinking water when your house is being sprayed with pesticides.

(vii) Pesticides can be absorbed through the skin. Do not touch pesticides with bare hands.

DROWNING

When a person is drowned water enters into the windpipe creating obstruction in the respiratory system. When a person is having trouble with his breathing:

(i) his lips, nails and tongue turn blue in colour;

(ii) his pulse is slow and irregular;

(iii) he may lose consciousness.

A person who has stopped breathing has only 4 minutes to live. Thus the first-aider has to act fast.

Treatment

(i) Always start mouth-to-mouth breathing at once before trying to get water out of the drowning person's stomach, and if possible even before the drowning person is out of the water, as soon as it is shallow enough to stand.

(ii) If you cannot blow air into his lungs, when you reach the shore, quickly put his head lower than his feet and push his belly. Then continue mouth-to-mouth breathing at once in the following ways:

Step-1 Quickly remove anything stuck in the mouth or throat. Pull the tongue forward. If there is mucus in the throat, quickly try to clear it out.

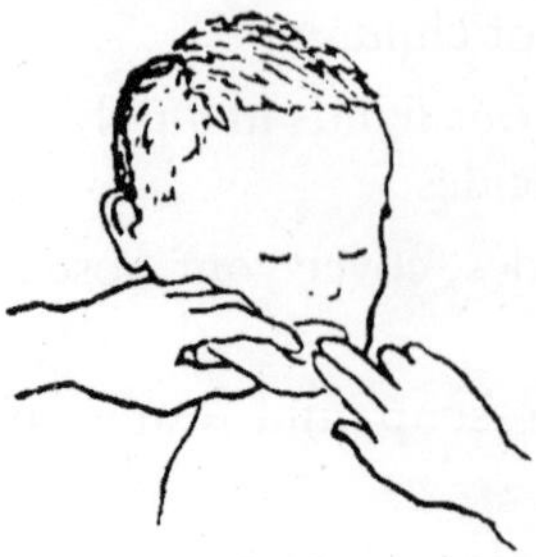

Fig. 1

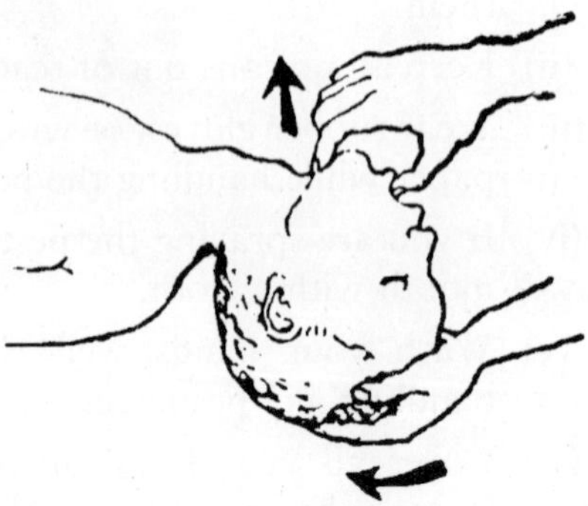

Fig. 2

Step-2 Quickly lay the person face up, tilt his head way back or pull his jaw forward.

Step-3 Pinch his nostrils closed with your fingers, open his mouth wide, cover his mouth with yours, and blow strongly into his lungs so that his chest rises, pause to let the air come back out and blow again. Repeat about 15 times per minute. With new born babies, breaths very gently about 25 times per minute.

Fig. 3

Continue mouth-to-mouth breathing until the person can breathe by himself, or until there is no doubt he is dead.

Sometimes you must keep it up for an hour or more.

(iii) Make the drowned child lie along the belly. Raise him by putting your hands below near the belly. Keep on holding him in this position till the water comes out.

(iv) After the whole water comes out and after normal respiration is resumed, the wet clothes of the victim should be removed and dry clothes should be provided, body should be covered with warm clothes.

(v) Stimulants like hot milk, coffee, tea should be given if the victim is in a position to drink.

SUNSTROKE

Sunstroke is not common, but is very dangerous. It occurs especially in older people and alcoholics during hot weather. Sunstroke is otherwise known as heat stroke.

Signs of Sunstroke

(i) The skin is dry, red and hot.

(ii) The person has a very high fever, sometimes more than 42°C.

(iii) The person is very ill or unconscious.

Treatment

(i) Put the person in the shade.

(ii) Take off his clothes and pour cold water over him.

(iii) Fan him.

(iv) Give ice cold water enema.

(v) Take the temperature every 10 minutes.

(vi) When the temperature comes down to 38°, stop pouring cold water on him.

(vii) Seek medical help.

Precaution

To avoid sunstroke always drink plenty of water with salt throughout the day in summer. Cover your head with a piece of cloth or umbrella when you are required to go out.

BURNS

Burns are caused in different ways. A burn is caused by dry heat or flame. A scald is caused by steam or hot liquid. Chemical burns are produced by the chemical action on the skin. Electric burns are caused by electric flash which damages the skin. The dangers from burns are shock and infection. Burns are classified into three categories according to the damage done as follows:

1st degree: Miner burns that do not form blisters.

2nd degree: Burns that cause blisters.

3rd degree: Deep burns that destroy the skin and expose raw flesh.

Prevention

Most burns can be prevented. Take special care with children:

(i) Do not let small babies go near fire.

(ii) Keep lamps and matches out of reach.

(iii) Turn handles of pans on the stove so that children cannot reach them.

Treatment

(i) To help ease the pain and lesson damage caused by a minor burn, put the burned part in cold water at once. No other treatment is needed.

(ii) Give aspirin to relieve pain.

(iii) If the burn has formed blisters, do not break blisters. If the blisters are broken, wash gently with soap and boiled water that has been cooled, Sterilize a little Vaseline by heating it until it boils and spread it on a piece of sterile gauze. Then put the gauze on the burn. If there is no Vaseline, put some cotton violer, leave the burn uncovered.

(iv) It is very important to keep the burn as clean as possible. Protect it from dirt, dust, and flies.

(v) If signs of infection appear—pus, bad smell, fever or swollen lymph nodes—apply compresses of potassium permanganate solution 3 times a day. If potassium permanganate is not available, you can use warm salt water (1 teaspoon salt to 1 litre water). Boil both the water and cloth before use. With great care remove the dead skin and flesh. You can spread on a little antibiotic such as Neosporin. In severe cases, consider taking an antibiotic such as pencillin or ampicillin by mouth.

(vi) In case of deep burn, take the person to a health centre at once. In the meantime, wrap the burned part with a very clean cloth or towel.

(vii) Never put greese, fat, hides, coffee, herbs, or feces on a burn.

Special precautions for very serious burns

Any person who has been badly burned can easily go into shock—because of combined pain, fear and loss of the body fluids from the burn. What is needed is to comfort and reassure the burned person. Give him Paracetamol for the pain. Bathing open wounds in slightly salty water also helps calm pain. Put 1 teaspoon of salt for each litre of boiled (and cooled) water. Give the burned person plenty of liquid. If the burned area is large, make up the following drink:

To a liter of water add half a teaspoon of salt, and half a teaspoon of bicarbonate of soda.

Also put in 2 or 3 table-spoons of sugar or honey and some orange or lemon juice if possible.

BITES

(a) Animal bite

Puncture wounds inflicted by pets or stray animals occasionally cause severe infection. Rabies may result from a mammal bite, especially a dog bite. Cats, rats and squirrels may also be carriers of the rabies virus. The offending mamal should be kept under observation until it is determined that it is not suffering from rabies. The wound should be cleaned with soap and water and a sterile dressing applied. Obtain medical attention for rabies immunization at once even though the wound is minor. One should never wait to see if trouble develops.

(b) Snake bite

All snakes are not poisonous, nor can they outrun man as commonly believed. There are only four common poisonous snakes in India:

1. Cobra,
2. Krait,
3. Russel's viper,
4. Saw-scaled viper.

When a person has been bitten by a snake, try to find out if the snake was poisonous, or not. Their bite marks are different. The bite of a poisonous snake leaves marks of the 2 fangs (and at rare times, other little marks made by the teeth). The bite of a snake that is not poisonous leaves only 2 rows of teeth marks but no fang marks. Most often the bite marks are not so clear. There may be just one fang mark, or just a row of teeth marks, or a ragged tear at the site of the wound. When in doubt, always look for the local and general signs of poison and keep the person under observation for at least one day.

Signs of Poisonous Snake Bite

At the site of snake bite: Local signs

These signs appear within 15 to 30 minutes of the bite:

(i) Pain—may be quite severe and may last for many days.

(ii) Swelling—depends upon the amount of poison that has entered the blood. In case of viper bites, pain and swelling at the site of the bite are more severe.

(iii) Bleeding from the bite—this is more common in case of viper bite.

(iv) Discolouration of the skin around the area of the bite.

(v) Infection and gangrene may also develop.

General Sings

These signs develop from 15 minutes to one hour after the bite.

I Cobra and Krait affect the nervous system:

(i) Drowsiness.

(ii) Weakness of the muscles, especially the muscles around the eyes.

(iii) Paralysis of muscles.

(iv) Respiratory failure may lead to death.

II Vipers affect the clotting of blood:

(i) Headache-giddiness.

(ii) Nausea, vomiting.

(iii) Cough with blood stained phlegm.

(iv) Bleeding under the skin.

(v) Signs of shock if there is too much bleeding.

Treatment for Poisonous Snake Bite

(i) Stay quiet. Do not move the part that has been bitten. The more it is moved, the more rapidly the poison will spread through the body. A person who has been bitten on the foot should not walk, not even one step if it can be avoided. Carry him on a stretcher.

(ii) Tie a cloth around the limb, just above the bite. Do not tie very tight, and loosen it for a moment every half hour.

(iii) With a very clean knite (sterilized in a flame) make a cut into each fang mark about 1 cm. long and 1/2 cm. deep.

(iv) Then suck (spit out) the poison for a quarter hour. If more than half hour has passed since the bite, do not cut or suck the bite. By then it may do more harm than good.

(v) If a person develops any of the general signs, inject ANTIVENIN. Be careful about the instruction that comes with the medicine. Inject 1/2 cc. of ADRENALINE under the skin to prevent the person from getting allergic shock. The antivenin is most effective if you inject it within 3 hours after the bite. For some snakes like cobra it must be given immediately.

(vi) If you can get ice, wrap pieces in thick cloth and pack these around the limb that was bitten.

(vii) Give tetanus toxoid injection to prevent tetanus.

(viii) If signs of infection develop, use pencillin.

(ix) Poisonous snake bite is dangerous. Send for medical help at once—but always do the things explained above at once.

Wounds (Caused by Sharp Instruments)

A wound is a break in the skin which permits the escape of blood. Break in the skin may be produced by knife, stone, sharp instruments or parts of the machinery. Wounds may be classified as:

- Abrasion (scraped),

- Incision (cut),
- Laceration (torn),
- Puncture wounds (stab),

The dangers that might complicate wounds are infection, hemorrhage and shock.

Treatment

(i) In the first-aid treatment of wounds cleanliness is very essential otherwise infection may occur. Do not touch the wound with hand or fingers or any unsterile material.

(ii) Minor wounds should be cleaned thoroughly with soap and warm water.

(iii) Then apply some antiseptic over the wound.

(iv) Dress the injured part with sterile gause and roller bandage. A fresh cloth thoroughly washed with soap and hot water and freshly ironed may be also used for bandage.

(v) If bleeding occurs all that is needed is direct pressure over the wound with sterile gauze or a clean unused handkerchief.

(vi) You may allow fresh water to run over the bleeding wound before applying pressure.

(vii) If severe bleeding occurs, the chief duty of the first-aider is to stop the loss of blood. Determine as quickly as possible the source of bleeding and apply direct pressure close to the wound, but not on the wound's edge. If direct pressure does not stop bleeding, it may be necessary to do the following:

- Keep pressing on the wound.
- Keep the wounded part as high as possible.
- Tie the arm or the leg as close to the wound as possible between the wound and the body. Tighten enough to control the bleeding. Do not make it so tight that the arm or leg becomes blue.

- For the tie, use a folded cloth or a wide belt, never use thin rope, string or wire.
- Loosen the tie for a moment every half hour to see if it is still needed and to let the blood circulate. Leaving it too long may damage the arm or leg so much that it must be cut off.
- Never use dirt, cowdung, kerosene, or coffee to stop bleeding.
- Raise the feet and lower the head to prevent shock.
- Seek medical help.

SAFETY

1. What is Safety?

Safety means freedom from danger, accidents, injury or any hazard. To be safe means to remain protected from danger, to remain unhurt or uninjured. In modern day living accidents and common injuries are inevitable unless the individual remains careful, unless the physical environment is designed properly and unless safety measures are followed in the school at home and on the road. If the physical environment in the school and at home is designed properly, and if individuals follow certain safety measures, hazards and dangers which occasionally occur in the school, home or on the road can be eliminated or atleast reduced.

2. Safety Measures at Home

Babies and very young children have a natural desire to understand their environment. They like to manipulate objects, to touch, smell, hold, throw any object that is within their reach. Their curiosity to know about the world coupled with their immaturity to manipulate their physical environment and their ignorance about the objects very often lead to injuries and accidents. Parents and other older members in the family have an important role to play in ensuring safety measures at home:

(i) All fire—from the coal, gas, electricity or wood should be protected to prevent babies and young children from getting their hands through it.

(ii) Unused match boxes and match sticks should be kept out of reach of children.

(iii) Pots and pans containing hot water, hot milk, hot tea or hot oil should be kept away from the reach of young children.

(iv) Use of iron box, table lamps, fans and other electrical appliances should be made cautiously.

(v) Protect children from playing with sharp instruments like knife, scissors and parts of machines.

(vi) Take precautions while using pesticides. Wear rubber gloves, or wrap your hands in a polythene paper while handling pesticides. If you are spraying presticides, cover your nose and mouth with a cloth. Wash your hands well with soap and water after handling any pesticides. Cover all your food and drinking water when your house is being sprayed with pesticides. Ask children to remain out while pesticides are being sprayed.

(vii) Never keep kerosene, gasoline, or other poisons in cola or soft drink bottles, because children may try to drink them.

(viii) Keep all poisons out of reach of children.

(ix) All medicines should be kept in a place out of reach of children.

(x) Do not take overdose of medicines. Never use a medicine unless you are sure about its use.

(xi) Be very careful about home remedies prescribed by relatives and neighbours.

(xii) Take care of slippery bathrooms, dark passages or corner in the home and while throwing skins of bananas and fruits. Such cases may lead to fracture dislocation, sprains, bites, etc.

(xiii) Don't let young children play with fire works and stand or sit close to fire works on festive occasions. If you cannot restrict them, remain with them and guide them every moment.

(xiv) Tell children not to touch abandoned objects—boxes, bags, tins, etc., to prevent them from being victims of bomb blast.

(xv) Don't entertain strangers in your home, ask children to avoid strangers who may appear pleasant and friendly outwardly.

3. Safety Measures in the School

Safety measures in the school are as important as safety measures at home. Most of the injuries and accidents that occur in the school are those that occur during recreation and leisure hours, just before and after the school hour and in play grounds and occasionally in laboratories. Some of these injuries and accidents occur due to mischief, foul play, lack of precaution necessary to handle equipments and disobedience. The school authorities can take the following safety measures to prevent injuries and accidents:

(i) If the school is very close to the main road, it must have a compound wall with a gate to prevent children going out of the compound to the road during play time and likely to face accidents. The gate must always remain closed except during beginning and closing hours. If the school does not have a compound wall or a gate some one in the school must keep an eye on the movements of young children.

(ii) If there are trees in the school compound children should be prevented from climbing the trees.

(iii) Care must be taken to see that there are no slippery grounds or paths in the school.

(iv) The physical education teacher must ensure proper discipline in the playground. Children should be discouraged to throw stones at one another, pull or push other children or play fool plays during play time. Every child should be asked to obey rules and regulations of play.

(v) Children should be asked to use pencil-cutters and not blades to sharpen their pencils.

(vi) The playground must be kept clean. All pieces of glass, sharp edged stones or sticks should be collected and removed from the playground every day.

(vii) In laboratory and science periods all precautions should be taken to prevent any hazard or danger.

(viii) Children should be discouraged to put pencil ends, pen caps, geometrical equipments, cycle balls, chalks, etc., in to the mouth, nose or ears. This may cause serious dangers.

4. Safety on the Road

Now-a-days the number of accidents on the road is extremely more than it was 5 to 10 years back. On many occasions accidents take place due to sheer carelessness. School-going children who do not know the rules of the road and cross the road from one side to the other face accidents. If a child is taught to take a pause and look to both sides before stepping into the road and if he finds that the elderly people are doing so, automatically a habit will be formed in him which can prevent accidents. Hence from the very beginning training on safety measures should be given to the children. To prevent accidents on the road the following steps may be considered:

(i) Small children do not know the rules of the road. Until they are conscious of this thing, they should not be allowed to go to the busy roads alone. Some elder member of the family should accompany them in case of necessity.

(ii) Sometimes while playing football, volley ball or cricket, the ball rolls down the road near the playground of the school. Students generally go in a hurry to get the ball and face accidents. Therefore they should not be allowed to go in hurry. Even at times students play on the road. This should also be restricted.

(iii) Children should be taught about the rules of crossing the road. They should remember the following important facts:

(a) Not to cross the road until it is clear. Look to both the sides while crossing the road.

(b) Go straight across. Not to cross at an angle.

(c) Walk quickly but do not run.

(d) Watch the buses and cars, etc.

(e) Always obey traffic light signals; if the light is red do not cross. Wait until the light is turned into green.

(iv) Walk on the footpath if it is available. If there is no footpath they should be instructed to walk on the left-side of the road keeping close to the side.

(v) While using a bus or a tram, children should remember the following things:

(a) Not to get in until the passengers have got off.

(b) Not to get down until the bus has stopped.

(c) After getting down not to cross the road until the bus has moved.

(vi) The children should be taught to obey the signs of the traffic police in order to prevent accidents.

7

Posture

Children perform various activities every day. They read, sit, stand, walk, write and play. While performing these activities they have to hold their body in specific positions depending upon the nature of the activity performed at a given time. Posture refers to that accustomed position which enables the body to function efficiently. Good posture leads to good health and more energy for activity.

Posture is an attitude of mind to hold the body in a way to facilitate work. Different works require different posture. Thus we have sitting posture, standing posture, walking posture, reading posture and writing posture. Posture is maintained as a matter of habit which is largely due to learning. Thus parents and teachers should teach children about correct postures and the evil effects of defective postures.

1. CORRECT POSTURAL HABIT OF STANDING

A good standing posture should be easy and effortless, otherwise it is unlikely to be maintained as a habit. In the correct standing position, the body should be kept erect, and balanced without any discomfort, and the weight of the body should be equally divided on both the legs. The heels should rest on the flat surface correctly and no muscle should be strained. The body should be held up-right, the chest out, the shoulders in a straight line and the abdomen in. While standing, the knecs should be kept straight, legs placed some-what apart, body should be kept straight, body should not be bent forward but held erect, arms should hang straight by the sides of the body and hips should be drawn back.

But such an ideal position of attention cannot be maintained for a longer period. So the best device is to put one foot in advance of the other causing the other foot to support weight of the whole body. The muscles of the forward leg are thus relaxed. When one leg gets tired, the position may be varied and the other leg put forward. Thus both the legs get rest alternately. Thus the position is called standing position at ease.

In short, good standing position may be outlined as follows:

(i) Abdomen retracted and the lower part flat.

(ii) Arms hanging comfortably at the sides.

(iii) Body weight balanced over balls of the feet.

(iv) Chest evated but nut puffed out.

(v) Facial expression of alertness.

(vi) Feet parallel.

(vii) Head erect and facing the front.

(viii) Hips level and drawn back slightly.

(ix) Knees straight but at ease.

(x) Shoulder blades flat.

(xi) Spinal curves within normal limits.

(xii) Well-balanced body, alert, yet confortable.

2. CORRECT POSTURAL HABIT OF WALKING

While walking, one should move straight as far as possible. The body should be vertical to the ground. Hands should be swinged properly. When the right leg moves forward, the left hand must be swinged backward and vice-versa. While walking, one should not be in a hurry. One should not also walk too long at a stretch. There should be proper limit and speed in walking. Unrestricted speady walking may cause unwanted accidents.

3. CORRECT POSTURAL HABIT OF SITTING

In a good sitting posture the body should be held-up-right to give freedom for the chest to expand and to prevent restriction and pressure on the abdominal organs. In sitting upright without proper support the child may become tired quickly. Therefore the body in the sitting position requires to be supported by the back rest, the seat and the floor. The seat should be of a definite form to aid-up right postures. The back

Which one is the correct posture of sitting?

rest should be shaped to support the back and should hold it firmly just below the shoulder blades. The feet should be flat on the floor, slightly apart and parallel. That is why the seat must be accurately fixed for the needs of the child. It is not desirable to sit with a bent vertebral column. The hip region should be properly placed at the sitting place. The head, shoulders and hips should be in a straight line.

4. CORRECT POSTURAL HABIT OF READING

1. *Good posture.* The chair back is shaped to fit into the lumbar spine.
2. *And* 4. The trunk has slipped forward, so that the weight comes increasingly on the end of the spine and the chest and abdominal organs are cramped. Part of the bad effects of 4 is due to the chair which is too low.
3. Though the body is well back on the seat, the longs and the viscera are probably impeded.

In reading, the book should be inclined at an angle of 60° and should be placed at a distance of 30 cm from the eyes so that the pressure on the eyes may be minimum. Wrong postures for reading are the potent causes of short-sight, contracted chest, stretched muscles of the back and deformity. For reading purpose, the body should be prevented as it may cause eye trouble. The head should be kept erect, thighs horizontal, legs vertical and feet should rest flat on the ground.

Effect of different sitting Postures for reading

(*Source:* Davies, M.B.: *Hygiene and Health Education for Training Colleges.*)

Stooping and bending of head should be kept well-balanced between the shoulders. For easy reading an angle of 45° should be formed between the eyes and the hand holding the book. Book of bold prints should be given to the young children for reading. Books with small size printing should be avoided especially for small children.

Four sitting postures are usually noticed among children while reading a book. Among these four postures, posture No. 1 is good and ideal for reading.

5. CORRECT POSTURAL HABIT OF WRITING

The position of the seat is very important for the purpose of writing. While writing, the body must be held up-right. To avoid physical defects the writing slope of the desk must not be too distant from the seat. At the time of writing, the edge of the slope most rest almost at the abdomen. The height of the writing slope from the floor should be such that writing arms can be placed comfortably on the slope without raising the shoulder or stooping forward. The height should not be too high or too low. While writing only the hands will move but not the arms. The writer must sit up-right and his back be supported by the back of the seat properly. The shoulders should be kept parallel to the edge of the desk. His weight should be evenly distributed over the seat. The writer should not drop forward but may slightly bow down.

Writing requires co-ordination of a larger number of small muscles and hence involves a great strain. In order to release that strain children adopt all sorts of wrong postures. This should be prevented by correct writing posture:

(a) (b)

(a) Economical good writing position, with the chair drawn-up under the desk, the seat fully supporting the thigh, the feet firmly on the floor, not dangling, and the shoulder weight partly supported by the left arm.

(b) Uneconomical bad writing posture. The chair is too far from the desk and the thighs unsupported. The trunk is cramped and not erect. The chest is contracted, producing round shoulders and increased likelihood of respiratory diseases.

[*Source*: Davies, M.B. *Hygiene and Health Education for Training Colleges*]

For writing, the paper should be placed square with the desk and directly in front of the pupil. The right arm should rest comfortably on the desk and the hand lightly on its side. The support provided in this way, the hand, wrist and little finger will not only make writing less fatiguing but give freedom of movement to the pen. The muscles of the fingers should not be strained in grasping the pen. A light easy hold gives freedom of movement. The left arm should help to support the body and is needed to keep the paper firm for writing.

6. COMMON POSTURAL DEFECTS

Some common postural defects of young children are as follows:

Postural Defects of Standing

(i) The body does not remain erect, balanced, and symetrical.

(ii) The weight of the body is not equally divided on both sides of the legs as a result one leg remains erect and the other leg slightly bends forward.

(iii) The chest is pushed little backward.

(iv) The shoulders do not remain in a straight line.

(v) The abdomen is pushed out.

Postural Defects of Walking

(i) Pressure either on the front part of the foot or the toes.

(ii) Walking in a hurry.

(iii) The body does not remain vertical to the ground but bends forward.

(iv) Hands do not swing properly.

Postural Defect of Sitting

(i) The body is not held up-right.

(ii) The head, shoulders and hips are not in a straight line.

(iii) Pressure is on the abdominal organs.

(iv) The body is not supported by back-rest.

(v) The feet do not remain flat on the floor, slightly apart and parallel.

(vi) The body bends forward or to one side.

Postural Defects of Reading

(i) The book is placed too close or too far from the eyes.

(ii) Most of the common defects of sitting are noticed.

(iii) Stooping and bending of head.

Postural Defects of Writing

(i) Improper gap between the edge of the slope and the abdomen.

(ii) Shoulder raised.

(iii) Stooping forward or to one side.

(iv) Defective sitting postures.

(v) Weight of the body not evenly distributed over the seat.

(vi) Writing paper not placed square with the desk and not directly in front of the writer.

(vii) Pressure on the hands and wrist.

(viii) Finger muscles strained.

7. CAUSES OF COMMON POSTURAL DEFECTS

Defects in postural habits are caused by a number of factors such as:

(i) Poor nutrition,

(ii) Organic strains,

(iii) Hidden diseases,

(iv) Low physical fitness,

(v) Sedentary living,

(vi) Chronic fatigue,

(vii) Hearing and visual defects,

(viii) Emotional disturbances,

(ix) Ignorance and lack of guidance about correct postural habits and evil effects of bad postures,

(x) Improper desks and chairs.

Other things being equal, the way the child feels at any moment, conditions in the home and the school, attitude of parents and teachers to child's postural habits—all these contribute to defective postural habits of children.

8. EVIL EFFECTS OF DEFECTIVE POSTURAL HABITS

According to Carl E. Willgose (1979), defects in postural

habits of children lead to deviations in appearance and behaviour. These deviations in appearance and behaviour are as follows:

(i) Flabby musculature,
(ii) Chronic fatigue,
(iii) Round Shoulders,
(iv) Head forward,
(v) One shoulder lower than the other,
(vi) Pratruding shoulder blades,
(vii) Pigeon or funnel chest,
(viii) Lateral curvature of spine,
(ix) Unequal height of hips,
(x) Irregular gait in walking,
(xi) Arches of feet are flat,
(xii) Feet toe—out too far in standing/walking,
(xiii) Tendon above heel bone is bowed inward when standing,
(xiv) Heels of shoes wear down on inside borders,
(xv) Pain in joints of body,
(xvi) Pain in bones of foot.

9. ROLE OF THE TEACHER IN CORRECTING DEFECTIVE POSTURES AND TEACHING GOOD POSTURES

Childhood is the formative years of life. It is during this stage that god habits can be learned well and bad habits can be broken easily. An important part of this period is spent in primary schools and junior secondary schools. The teacher has therefore, an important role to play in correcting defective posture of children and teaching them good postures:

(i) The teacher should possess good knowledge of different postures, causes of defective postures and evil effects of defective postures.
(ii) He should not only have knowledge about good postures but also demonstrate them in his daily life. Because young children have a tendency to initiate the teacher. If the teacher adopts defective postures of sitting, standing,

walking, reading and writing he cannot expect children to adopt good potures.

(iii) The teacher should be vigilant about the postural habits of children and correct their defects as and when observed.

(iv) He should impress upon the students about the importance of postures.

(v) In teaching good postures to students the following methods and approaches are found useful:

- Demonstration by the teacher in the class.
- Instruction by the P.E.T.
- Talk by doctors and specialists.
- Documentary film shows, slides, pictures.
- Demonstration by students.

(vi) The teacher can organise meeting of guardians in the school and discuss with them about postural habits and seek their co-operation in correcting defective postural habits of children.

(vii) Periodical medical examinations should be held in the school to identify and assess physical defects of children and help them to overcome such defects.

(viii) The school time-table should be modified or framed properly to reduce the effects of fatigue.

(ix) The teacher must ensure that the classroom furniture—chairs, desks, benches and tables are of the ideal size and height for the students.

(x) Open air classes may be organised at intervals to help students enjoy fresh air, sit on the ground and feel little free.

8

Communicable Diseases

Diagnosis of disease and prescription for its treatment are medical responsibilities and for teachers to attempt either would be both unwise and dangerous. But if a teacher possesses some knowledge of communicable diseases he can recognise the signs of illness at an early stage and make sure that advice is sought from doctors in good time and help to see that such advice is carried out sincerely.

1. MEANING OF COMMUNICABLE DISEASES

Communicable diseases are those which are caused by living germs which are transmitted or transferred from one person or animal to another person or animal. Such transmission may be by direct contact, or indirectly through the medium of household articles, clothing, toys, food, water or sewage, or by way of insect pests. Communicable diseases are of two types:

(i) *Contagious Diseases*: When the infection is transmitted by direct contact with infected persons or objects.

(ii) *Infectious Diseases*: When infection is transmitted through the pollution of some media like food, water or air.

Both the types have one thing in common. Infection occurs when disease producing germs gain entry to the body and multiply there.

Communicable diseases are different from an epidemic or endemic. An epidemic arises when a disease spreads rapidly attacking many people within a short span of time. Sometimes what began as an epidemic becomes an endemic. An endemic recurs continually in a particular area.

2. CAUSES OF COMMUNICABLE DISEASES

Each communicable disease is caused by a distinct type of germ or virus which is capable of causing that particular disease alone and no other disease. Thus the diphtheria germ causes diphtheria; the poliomyelitis virus causes poliomyelitis, but neither the one nor the other can cause typhoid fever. Germs are very small living things which are invisible to the naked eye. Germs need suitable conditions in respect of food, warmth and moisture for their growth and reproduction. Given such conditions, a single germ may multiply rapidly, producing many millions in 24 hours.

3. SPREAD OF COMMUNICABLE DISEASES

Three factors are necessary for the spread of communicable diseases:

(i) There must be a source of infection from which the germs are spread;

(ii) There must be a route by which they are transferred; and

(iii) There must be a region in which they are able to settle and grow (the body of a susceptible person).

The source of infection is always another person, or an animal in whom the particular type of germ has established itself. Usually the chief source of human infection is man himself. The "carrier" is another well-recognised source of infection. The "carrier" is a person who, without exhibiting in himself any symptoms of a communicable disease, is nevertheless harbouring the germs somewhere in his body, so that he is liable to spread them to others.

Animals and insects frequently act as sources of infection. For example, tuberculosis may be caused by the milk of a cow infected with this disease. Food poisoning may be caused by mice and flies. Similarly malaria is transmitted by certain kinds of mosquito.

There are several routes by which germs gain entry into the human body. They are generally spread in one or more of the following ways:

(i) Direct contact between the infected person and another person through bodily contact, coughing and sneezing. Many common diseases like cold, measles, whooping cough, ring work, tuberculosis, etc., are spread by direct contact.

(ii) Air — Infection is often spread by the process known as "droplet infection". When the infected person coughs, sneezes, talks, or shouts he propels into the air, for a distance of 3 to 6 feet, small drops of sputum which are laden with germs. The air of crowded places, classrooms, cinema halls and ill-ventilated houses is full of different kinds of germs. When this air is inhaled by a healthy person, germs get entry to his body and he is infected. Diphtheria, whooping cough, measles, influenza and common cold spread through air.

(iii) Food and drinks — Flies sit on exposed food and drink and deposit germs of various infectious diseases. Diseases like cholera, typhoid, dysentery and diarrhoea spread in this way.

(iv) Bites of insects — Certain insects transmit disease through bites on the skin. Malaria, yellow fever, plague, etc., spread in this way.

(v) Cuts in the skin — Germs enter the body through cuts in the skin and spread diseases like tetanus, rabies, etc.

(vi) Through genital passages — Germs of venereal disease gain access to the body via the genital passages. Diseases like syphilis and gonorrhoea may spread in this way.

Whatever route germs may use in entering the body, there is always an interval between the infection of the susceptible person and the appearance of actual symptoms in him. This interval is known as the incubation period.

Whether disease follows infection depends upon the number of germs, their virulence and the individual's power of resistance. The power to resist disease is known as immunity which varies from individual to individual and in the same individual at different times.

4. COMMON SYMPTOMS OF COMMUNICABLE DISEASES

Every communicable disease is caused by a specific germ or virus. Thus the symptoms also vary from disease to disease. But there are some symptoms which are common to all communicable diseases. These common symptoms are:

- Shivering;
- Rise in temperature;
- Routes in the skin;
- Headache;
- Nausea or vomiting;
- Sore throat.

5. PREVENTION OF COMMUNICABLE DISEASES

So far as communicable diseases are concerned, prevention is better than cure. The following measures are important:

(i) In the prevention of infection both the individual and the community have important roles to play.

(ii) In all cases of communicable diseases the local medical officer must be notified who will take all necessary steps to prevent or reduce the spread of diseases.

(iii) Infectious patients should be isolated in their own homes or if they are suffering from one of the more serious communicable diseases, in an infectious diseases hospital, where modern methods of treatment may bring about rapid cure. This will help to reduce the risk of infection being passed on to others.

(iv) Any one who has been in contact with cases of certain communicable diseases, such as small pox may be kept under observation for a period of time equal to the longest incubation period of the disease concerned.

(v) Children are susceptible to the more common infections. They may be advised to remain on leave after they are affected by infection. This will prevent spread of disease to other children in the school.

(vi) Any one concerned with milk production or with preparing food for public consumption who has been in contact with infectious diseases should be prevented from going on with his work until he is fully cured.

(vii) By means of disinfection an attempt can be made to destroy the germs producing the disease.

(viii) All discharges from the patient, as well as any articles used by him, may have to be disinfected daily. At the end of the illness his room and all articles and furnishings which may have been contaminated can be disinfected. Simpler methods of disinfection include washing with soap and hot water, exposure to sunlight and through ventilation, boiling handkerchiefs, crokery and cutlery after a preliminary washings, etc.

(ix) When small pox breaks out, vaccination may be offered to all who have been vaccinated a long time ago or not at all.

(x) Public health measures such as good housing, prevention of over-crowding, proper ventilation, supply of purified drinking water and pasteurized milk, efficient disposal of refuse and sewage, and the cleanliness and protection of our food supplies are most effective in controlling some of the communicable diseases.

(xi) Coughs and sneezes spread diseases. Thus, anyone who must cough or sneeze should have a handkerchief ready, with his face turned well away from other people. Paper handkerchiefs are best, because they can be burnt.

(xii) There is always a risk of infection from germs lurking in dust, whether on floor, furniture or bedding. Frequent use of soap and hot water for cleaning floors and other surfaces, and free access of light and air to all parts of the house will help greatly in removing or killing germs. Soap and hot water are excellent disinfectants.

6. SOME COMMUNICABLE DISEASES

1. Measles

Measles is so infectious that to prevent the spread of infection from one child to another at home or school is most difficult. It is caused by a virus which is spread by droplet infection. It is most contagious during the early stage. Mortality is highest among children under the age of two.

Symptoms: It usually begins with cold and dry cough, fever, running of nose and eyes, sneezing; the temperature may go high up to 104°. After about three days of the attack, large pink blotches appear on the skin, on the face, first seen on the forehead and then on the temples behind the ears and then on all over the body. The eyes get swollen.

Treatment

(i) Isolate the child from other children.

(ii) Protect the child from bright light.

(iii) Keep him in bed in a well ventilated room.

(iv) Keep his body clean by giving bed-bath or sponge bath.

(v) Give vaccine to the child and other children in the family to avoid infection.

Precautions in the school

(i) Exclude the child from the school for three weeks.

(ii) Close the school if it is in the form of epidemic.

(iii) Inform medical authorities to control it.

2. Whooping Cough

Whooping cough is a serious disease of young children. It is caused by a specific germ which spreads by droplet infection.

Symptoms

(i) The characteristic whoop is not always present and occasionally diagnosis may be difficult without resorting to laboratory tests.

(ii) It begins with cold, coughing, sneezing and fever.

(iii) Any cough accompanied by vomiting is suspicious.

(iv) For sometime there may be no suggestion that the child is suffering from anything more than an ordinary cold and cough. Yet it is at this stage that the disease is most infectious.

(v) The termination of the disease is also very indefinite.

The child may continue to whoop for weeks after ceasing to be infectious.

(vi) From about six weeks after the onset of the illness, or four weeks after the beginning of the characteristic cough, there is no longer any risk of the patient infecting other people.

(vii) Although deaths from whooping cough are not now common, the risk is very greater to infants under one year.

Treatment

(i) Keep the patient warm in bed with plenty of fresh air in the room.

(ii) Avoid chilling the patient.

(iii) Generally cough starts when the patient eats anything and he may vomit. Give him liquid food which can be easily digested.

(iv) Get the child vaccinated against whooping cough.

(v) Homeopathy can be applied.

(vi) Chloromycitin injection and capsules are useful.

(vii) Don't allow the child mix with other children to prevent spread of the disease for at least six weeks.

3. Influenza

Influenza is caused by a virus which enters the body through nose, mouth and even through eyes. The germs spread by sneezing, coughing and infected discharge from the mouth and nose.

Symptoms

(i) To begin with the person feels feverish, headache, bodyache, shivering and perspiration.

(ii) The temperature may go high up to 104° to 105°.

(iii) There is severe pain in the back.

(iv) The temperature comes down with perspiration.

(v) The patient feels physically exhausted and mentally depressed.

(vi) Throat becomes sore and nose gets blocked.

Treatment

(i) Keep the patient warm in bed.

(ii) Avoid chilling the patient.

(iii) Give liquid diet to the patient.

(iv) Medicated steam inhalation will relieve blocked nose and help in smooth breathing.

(v) Apply ice bag on the forehead to get rid of headache.

Precaution

(i) Isolate the child from other children.

(ii) Give separate utensils to the child.

(iii) If there is epidemic, close the school.

4. Small Pox

Small pox is a serious infectious disease. It attacks both children and adults. It is caused by specific virus. Its germs spread through breath, excretions and scabs from the skin. Infection lasts for at least six weeks till the skin is healed after every scab is cleared.

Symptoms

Small pox begins with a heavy chill, vomiting, intense headache, backache and rise in temperature. On the third day of the attach, rashes start appearing first on the forehead and afterwards spread all over the body. On the third day of appearance of the scabs, some clear watery fluid starts appearing in them and they look like blisters. After another three days, these blisters start getting depressed and the colour becomes dull yellow. After eight days fever will start diminishing and scabs also begin to dry. When the scabs fall off, they leave permanent marks on the face, body and even the eyes. If marks appear in the eye it causes blindness and if marks appear in the ear, it causes deafness.

Treatment

(i) Keep the patient in a dark room.

(ii) Keep him warm in bed.

(iii) If the temperature goes very high, use cold sponge.

(iv) Give liquid diet and plenty of water to the patient.

(v) Keep the bowels cleaned.

Precaution

(i) Donot allow the child to mix with others.

(ii) Isolate him and ask him not to attend school.

(iii) Apply vaccination to all members of the family.

(iv) Report to the local medical officer.

5. Malaria

Malaria is a very common disease which is spread by the bite of female mosquito. Since mosquitoes take birth in large number during rainy season, this disease is very common during rainy season.

Symptoms

(i) The patient has high temperature.

(ii) He suffers from headache, cold and shivering.

(iii) He feels excessive weakness.

(iv) There is lot of perspiration.

Treatment

(i) It is very necessary to kill the mosquitoes. Breeding places of mosquitoes such as drainages, ponds, and dirty places should be disinfected and sprayed with DDT.

(ii) The patient should be subject to blood test to confirm malaria.

(iii) If malaria is confirmed tablets such as camoquin, chloroquine should be given to the patient as per advice of the doctor.

(iv) Mosquito net should be used at right.

(v) The surrounding environment should be kept clean and hygienic.

(vi) The patient should be given complete rest.

6. Tuberculosis

Tuberculosis in man is caused either by the human or tubercle bacillus. People who suffer from active tuberculosis of the lungs spray infected droplets into the air as they talk or cough. These droplets are often inhaled directly into the air passages and lungs of other people, or else they may fall on the ground. Where they dry up and become part of the dust of our surroundings. Cows, infected with tuberculosis pass tubercle bacillus into milk which is then passed on to man when he drinks that milk. Tuberculosis is also caused by dusty and damped atmosphere, malnutrition, chain smoking, too much of alcoholic indulgence, too much of worries, childhood marriage and producing more children.

Symptoms

(i) Fever and night sweats.

(ii) Cough and pain in chest.

(iii) Loss of weight.

(iv) Loss of appetite.

(v) Fatigue and palpitation at slight exertion.

(vi) Rapid pulse rate.

Treatment and Precautions

(i) Early detection is very important to check the spread of the disease.

(ii) X-ray examination of the chest is useful for correct diagnosis.

(iii) B.C.G. vaccination produces good resistance to the disease.

(iv) Living places should be kept clean and free from smoke, dust and dirt.

(v) The patient should be kept free from hard work and worry.

(vi) The sputum and excreta of the patient should be burnt properly.

(vii) Regular morning and evening walks are very useful.

Bibliography

Aggarwal, J.C. (1993). *Development and Planning of Modern Education*, New Delhi, Vikash.

Dash, M. (1983). *Leadership Behaviour of Head Teachers*-Paper presented to Department of Psychology, Moray House College of Education, Edinburgh for DPTT.

Dash, M. (1984). *MLC in EVS*-Paper presented to the Department of Geography, MHCE, Edinburgh for DPTT.

Dash, M. (1984). *School Management by Objectives*-Papers presented to the Department of Educational Management, MHCE, Edinburgh for DPTT.

Dash, M. (1999). *Health, Physical Education and Recreation*, Cuttack, S.N. Book Store.

Dash, M. (2005). *Education in India—Problems and Perspectives*, New Delhi, Atlantic Publishers and Distributors (P) Ltd.

Dash, M., et al. (1997). *Secondary School Organisation, Education Technology and Guidance*, Cuttack, S.N. Book Store.

Dash, M.R., Nanda, G.C. (1997). *Trends and Issues in Indian Education*, Cuttack, S.N. Book Store.

Dash, Neena (2004). "Is Teaching a Profession?" EDUTRACKS, Vol. 4, No. 4.

Dash, Neena (2005). "Changing Role of the Teacher." EDUTRACKS, Vol. 4, No. 7.

Gall, Nicholas (1978). *Foundations and Principles of Health Education*, New York, John Wiley.

Government of Himachal Pradesh, *Education Code*.

Haag, J.H. (1980), *School Health Education Programme*. New Delhi, Oxford & IBH.

HMSO (1966). *School Health Education*. Education Pamplet, No. 31, London.

Kilander, H.F. (1970). *School Health Education,* London, MacMillan.

Ministry of Education, Govt. of India. *Report of Secondary Education Commission* (1954), New Delhi.

Ministry of Education, Govt. of India. *Report of Education Commission* (1966), New Delhi.

MHRD, Govt. of India. *National Policy of Education* (1986), New Delhi.

Mukhopadhyay, M. (2001). *Total Quality Management in Education*, New Delhi, NIEPA.

Travers, J.P. (1982). *Educational Psychology*, New York, Harper & Row.